Kingdom Parables in Jewish Soil

By R. Darrell Wallace

© 2025 Spiritbuilding Publishers.
All rights reserved. No part of this book may be reproduced in any form without the written permission of the publisher.

Published by
Spiritbuilding Publishers
9700 Ferry Road, Waynesville, Ohio 45068

KINGDOM PARABLES IN JEWISH SOIL
By R. Darrell Wallace

All Scripture quotations, unless otherwise indicated, are taken from the Holy Bible, New International Version. Copyright 1973, 1978, 1984 International Bible Society. Used by permission of Zondervan Publishing House. *All rights reserved.*

ISBN: 978-1-964-80525-2

Spiritbuilding
PUBLISHERS

spiritbuilding.com

Table of Contents

Dedication 1
About the Author 2
The Author's Encouragement 2
How to Use This Book 3
Introduction 4

Part 1

Chapter 1   The Teaching Style of the Rabbis 8
Chapter 2   Approaching the Sacred Text: A First-Century Jewish
            Hermeneutic 16
Chapter 3   The Jewish Concept of the Kingdom of God 23
Chapter 4   The Reign of God in the Old Testament 28
Chapter 5   Guidelines for Explaining the Parables 37

Part 2

Chapter 6   Kingdom Parables in Jewish Soil 41
Chapter 7   The Parable of the Sower 47
Chapter 8   The Parable of the Seed 53
Chapter 9   The Parable of the Weeds in the Field 59
Chapter 10 Kingdom of Heaven and Kingdom of Their Father 69
Chapter 11 The Parables of the Mustard Seed and the Yeast 78
Chapter 12 The Parable of the Hidden Treasure and the
            Pearl of Great Price 85
Chapter 13 The Parable of the Dragnet 91
Chapter 14 The Parable of the House Owner 96

Part 3

Chapter 15 The Parable of the Merciful King, Part 1 103
Chapter 16 The Parable of the Merciful King, Part 2 111
Chapter 17 The Parable of the Workers in the Vineyard 117
Chapter 18 The Parable of the Royal Wedding Banquet, Part 1 . . . 123
Chapter 19 The Parable of the Royal Wedding Banquet, Part 2 . . . 132
Chapter 20 The Murdered Son and a Rejected Stone 139
Chapter 21 The Parable of the Ten Maidens 145
Chapter 22 The Parable of the Talents 154

Part 4

Chapter 23 The Kingdom of the Messiah Is the
 Restored Kingdom of Israel 163

Bibliography 172
Endnotes 175

Dedication

To my wife, Robin, whose love and prayers sustain me and through whom
God has demonstrated his Reign,
teaching me how to be a better servant.

To my grandmother, who is now resting with her Lord.
Her genuine faith was passed to her children and grandchildren
before she entered eternity the day after her 98th birthday.

About the Author

Darrell Wallace earned his Bachelor's in Biblical Studies from Sunset International Bible Institute in Lubbock, Texas. Since graduating from SIBI in 1989, he has served as an evangelist for four congregations in Kentucky and as Interim Director of Athens International Bible Institute in Athens, Greece. Darrell also served as a shepherd in the church. Presently, he is the Director of Teacher Recruitment and Training at the World English Institute. In 1980, he married Robin. They have two children who are now married and serving the Lord faithfully. Darrell and Robin have two wonderful grandchildren and currently live in Kentucky.

The Author's Encouragement

This work on the subject is not definitive; it is a work in progress. Take from it what you find useful, add to your study what you find lacking, and discard the rest. Although some errors are mentioned, this study is not an attempt to address them or enter into debate. It is intended to challenge some of our thoughts on the Kingdom Parables. I hope you will enjoy this study of the Kingdom Parables from a rarely studied angle.

R. Darrell Wallace

How to Use This Book

This book may be used for personal study or small group studies on your own timeline. However, if churches want to use it for class material, it can be done in two quarters. There are 23 lessons. However, some chapters have such detail that they could be studied over two or three weeks, lengthening the study and filling the remaining three weeks in the two quarters. This is just a suggestion. Please feel free to use however best benefits you and your group. Each chapter ends with questions to serve as food for thought.

Introduction

Men like Adolf Jülicher, C.H. Dodd, Joachim Jeremias, and Kenneth Bailey have brought attention to the Jewishness of the parables of Jesus. It makes sense to study the parables through the Jewish culture of the late Second Temple period (200 B.C. to A.D. 70) since they were spoken by a Jewish rabbi to Jewish people. Bailey calls this *Oriental exegesis*. When examining a culturally conditioned text, Bailey recommends using "the standard critical tools of Western scholarship in combination with cultural insights gained from ancient literature, contemporary peasants, and Semitic versions." This approach can enhance our understanding of Jesus' parables from a first-century Jewish perspective. I have come to appreciate the Jewish quality of the early Christian community and am amazed at the immeasurable Jewish flavor found within the New Testament. I can confidently say it has opened new doors in my study of the Jewishness of the teachings of Jesus and the apostles.

To aid in my process of rediscovery, I began reading from other authors who had written from this perspective in the last seventy-five years or so. Despite being 2,000 years apart from the time of Christ, we are fortunate to have almost everything we need to gain insight into this subject. More than ninety percent of the Bible has shades and textures of Jewish expressions and idioms found in Jewish literature of the late Second Temple period and within the Dead Sea Scrolls. We also have a substantial amount of reputable and scholarly research in print today on Jewish-Christian beginnings. This makes the pursuit of the subject well within reach. If you decide to put in the effort, this new perspective will allow you to better understand the lifestyle of Jesus, the nature of God's Kingdom, how God's reign is demonstrated, and the importance placed on the two great commandments that summarize all of God's commandments. I was not expecting the freshness and rich understanding of these two great commandments as they relate to living within the Reign of God. You will enjoy being drawn by this study into what the Jews called the *Shema*, which is at the heart of the Torah. The *Shema* is God's love-mandate intended to center Israel's attention and affection upon God and his reign. It instructs, "Hear, O Israel, the

Lord our God, the Lord is one. And you shall love the Lord your God with all your heart and with all your soul and with all your mind and with all your strength." Alongside the *Shema* is its twin commandment, which we will refer to often in this study. "You shall love your neighbor as yourself." We will see that this love-mandate is where the Reign of God begins in the Christian life, just as it did in the life of the Hebrews. We will find this golden thread masterfully interwoven throughout the parables of the Kingdom.

Therefore, this book is the result of studying the Parables of the Kingdom in a fresh, new way. As expressed in the title, my approach will be to examine the Kingdom Parables of Christ in the light of their Jewish background. As you read, you will notice my frequent exchange of specific terms. For instance, rather than using the word Kingdom of God, I will predominantly use the phrase *Reign of God*. My purpose for this will become more evident as the study develops. Also, rather than using the word Law when referring to the five books of Moses, I will use the word *Torah*. The use of the word *Torah* is merely a way of reintroducing ourselves to the Jewish way of viewing the books of Moses. *Torah* means instruction or teaching. Many of us consider the Law of Moses as a legal system that was replaced by Christ. Indeed, Jesus did inaugurate a new covenant, and with it, "having canceled the charge of our legal indebtedness, which stood against us and condemned us; he has taken it away, nailing it to the cross" (Colossians 2:14). It is a careless and critical mistake to dismiss the Torah's continued importance to the new covenant and development of the Christian life, making it the foundation for the Reign of God. How unwise it would be to fail to learn from that which illuminated Israel's path throughout her history as a nation. I will also be referring to the first Christians as Jewish Christians. This emphasis merely identifies the original community of Christ and does not insinuate a separate group of Christianity in the first century.

The Arrangement of the Book

I have undertaken to answer these questions. In Jewish terms of the late Second Temple period, what did the Kingdom Parables communicate? How is the Reign of God demonstrated and viewed from the Kingdom

Parables? What would Jesus have us to know from these parables that transcend time and culture?

Chapter 1 discusses the teaching style of the rabbis of Jesus' day. Jesus fits nicely into the model of a Jewish rabbi who communicated his message in the Hebrew tradition.

Chapter 2 examines the Jewish method of interpreting the sacred text. Our attention to this subject is to understand that Jesus employed much of the same hermeneutic (process of interpreting) to Scripture that was common in ancient Jewish times. We will learn that his use and purpose for speaking in parables was consistent with the function of rabbinic parables of the day. However, three central points that I hope will be appreciated pertain to the role many of the Kingdom Parables play in the observance of the Shema (the first and second commandments), one's subsequent response, and the only exception that deviates from first-century rabbinic patterns which is Jesus' Messianic identity.

Chapter 3 reviews the Jewish concept of the Kingdom of God. How did the Jews of the late Second Temple period interpret the Kingdom of God? This study is necessary to form a context for the Kingdom Parables. The Jewish perceptions and expectations of the Kingdom of Heaven and the coming age were fundamentally at the core of the hope of Israel.

Chapter 4 examines what the Old Testament teaches about the Reign of God. This chapter will reveal the multidimensional rule of a Sovereign God and how Jesus is the Sovereign Anointed One.

Chapter 5 will present several guidelines for studying the parables. We will attempt to avoid past errors.

With this as our foundation, Chapter 6 begins the study of the Kingdom Parables, beginning with those recorded in Matthew 13, Mark 4, and Luke 8.

Chapters Seven through 22 are studies of the parables that are said to be likened to the Reign or the Kingdom of God.

Finally, in Chapter 23 there is an expansion of the study of the Kingdom of God. We will examine where the Parables of the Kingdom ultimately leads us—the restoration of the Kingdom of God to Israel and our place in this reign of God. This study aims to elaborate more upon the nature of the Kingdom-church relationship, showing it as Israel's full expectation.

How to Use This Study Guide

I recommend doing the following to get the most out of this study.

1. Read the parables and their contexts from five different versions. Include in that collection two word-for-thought translations, such as the New Living Translation or the New International Version. Use your judgment when selecting. Include three versions considered word-for-word translations: the New King James Version, the English Standard Version, and the New American Standard Version. Take a few minutes to read the Introductions in these versions to learn each one's translation philosophy and method.
2. Using only the five versions you have chosen, and note the variations in translation.
3. After you have read from each of these and made notes of your own, choose a word-for-word translation to use as your text and use the others as references.
4. Follow the study guide with your version of choice. Read all Scripture references and answer the questions at the end of each lesson.

This study can be theologically technical, but I hope it will enhance the pursuit of the Reign of God in your life, as it most certainly continues to be in mine.

R. Darrell Wallace

Part 1

Chapter 1

The Teaching Style of the Rabbis

Our Western culture should thank God for preserving the Jewish people during the Second Temple period. Without their undying determination to preserve their identity as the people of God, we, in succeeding generations, would be left without a great light. Much of what we read as established cultural and religious norms in the Gospels took shape during this period. The world had made drastic changes during that time, insisting upon forcing its ways into Jewish life. The darkness of paganism sought to extinguish the ancient flame. But it was the sages of old and rabbis of the Jewish people who gave their lives (imperfect as they were) to preserve the teachings of the Torah, the writings, and the prophets and prepared the seedbed for Jesus to sow the seeds of the Kingdom. By the time Jesus came into the world, the Jewish people were ready for what the parables of the Kingdom revealed.

The Birth of the Parable

A fundamental belief of the Jews is that all truth was revealed to Moses at Mount Sinai in two parts: (1) written and (2) oral. When the prophets and the other writings came along, they were viewed as inspired but thought not to add anything more to what had already been revealed to Moses. By the time of Christ, oral traditions, called *Mishnah*, were developed as the primary standard for interpreting the first five books of the Hebrew Bible. The Mishnah is the heart of rabbinic commentary on how to apply the Torah to Jewish everyday life.

In Jesus' day, the Mishnah was not yet committed to writing but was alive and well as oral tradition. In the synagogue school and growing up as a boy in Nazareth, Jesus most certainly would have studied the oral traditions of the rabbis. He would have learned these ancient teachings from these traditions. He would have memorized whole sections of Scripture with their *Midrashim* (another genre of rabbinic interpretations), and he would have learned the morals taught from rabbinic parables. He would have also been familiar with the ancient Jewish method of determining the meanings of the Scriptures. When the Jews studied the Torah, they often openly questioned the text. What would have appeared to us to be an argument between two men in the synagogue was nothing more than a healthy discussion on the meaning of God's word. The Jews, then and now, believe that asking honest questions does not express doubt toward God or show disrespect for him. Instead, it expresses trust in God's ability to hold the answers and our struggle to find them. Jesus, the Son of God, would have devoted himself to studying the Torah in the same tradition. All of this would have been a fundamental part of his Jewish education. He was immersed in everything Jewish.

The Rabbinic Style of Teaching

To better understand the way Jesus taught, it is necessary to understand the method of teaching commonly practiced by the rabbis of Jesus' day. Jesus spoke out of the backdrop of his culture and in true Jewish style. Have you ever noticed as you read about the life of Christ from the Gospels that no one rejected *the way* he taught? Instead, *what* he taught was often met with resistance. The rabbis of the Second Temple period developed a standard form of teaching called in Hebrew, *Meshalim,* meaning parables. This teaching method originated from the rabbis' cultural and religious background, according to Brad Young. Jewish literature preserved from that period contains nearly five thousand rabbinic parables. This wealth of material has shed light on the Jewishness laden within the parables of Jesus. It has helped to clarify the various Jewish idioms and expressions that Jesus used. So, it should not surprise us to learn that over one-third of Jesus' teachings in the Gospels are recorded in this same Jewish tradition. Luke contains the most significant percentage by recording fifty-two percent of the Lord's teachings in parables. John contains at least two Hebrew-style parables—the Good Shepherd and the Vine and Branches.

The Hebrew teaching method that involved the use of parables was similar to storytelling or *Haggadah*. It gave the listener a vivid mental image combined with a dramatic form that made the meaning compelling and convincing. Hyperbole, or the exaggeration of details, was often used. Jesus made use of this frequently in his parables. For instance, it would be very unusual for all the guests to refuse an invitation, but this is what we read in the Parable of the Great Supper and the Parable of the Wedding Banquet. It is not likely that a sack of barley could guarantee a hundred percent germination or that one grain could produce a hundred times itself as in the Parable of the Sower. Exaggeration was used to capture the listener's attention and emphasize a particular point.

Teaching in parables was a style of teaching in which the Jews looked for parallels and patterns. They did this with almost everything. By comparing and contrasting, one could gain a deeper understanding of the subject. It drew the listener into the discovery process. We all love discovering things. Parables invite the listener to look for a deeper level of meaning. This form of teaching was common in the Old Testament with metaphors and similes that add description and even value. For example, in Genesis 49:9, we read, "You are a lion's cub, O Judah; you return from the prey, my son. Like a lion, he crouches and lies down, like a lioness—who dares to rouse him?" The comparison of Judah to a lion describes specific characteristics about him. Take Solomon's Book of Proverbs, for example, where many comparative sayings exist. For instance, Proverbs 4:18-19 reads, "The path of the righteous is like the first gleam of dawn, shining ever brighter till the full light of day. But the way of the wicked is like deep darkness; they do not know what makes them stumble."

Claus Westermann says the primary function of comparison was to pass a value judgment on human behavior, corresponding to what we call ethics. This technique is often presented as a question to the listener of the proverb, asking whether they accept the identification involved. If he agrees, he will act accordingly and receive the reward. If the listener disagrees, then he would act accordingly but suffer the consequences.

Defining a Parable

The Greek word translated parable is *parabole*. It means "to throw alongside something." The most common Sunday school definition says a parable is an earthly story with a heavenly meaning. Someone else has suggested that a parable is an earthly story with "heavy" meaning. Parables are simply stories or illustrations laid alongside recognizable and undeniable truths.

Most of the parables told by rabbis are in Hebrew, not in Aramaic. Therefore, we may assume that Jesus also spoke his parables in Hebrew before being translated into Greek. The difference between the Greek and the Hebrew, or Aramaic, regarding parables is significant. In its basic form, the Greek word is more restricted in its application. We in the West have often resorted to defining what is and is not a parable through the standard Greek definition handed down to us. For example, we might not consider the saying, "Physician heal yourself," as a parable, or the saying, "We like sheep have gone astray," as a parable. Because of their brevity, they do not fit into our concept of being parables. They need expansion. They need a story to have that cast-along-side-of characteristic. However, these are parables in the Hebrew sense of the word.

The idea of resemblance is often more pronounced and vivid with Hebrew and Aramaic parables. Hebrew parables cast a more distinctive image using many forms. In many ways, they are typological, like a shadow is to its reality. Joachim Jeremias says this qualifies the following as parables: a metaphor, proverb, riddle, allegory, or simile. A parable may also be visual. Jesus drew lessons from visual examples, such as a little child, a fig tree, or fields ready for harvest. Broadening our concept to match a first-century concept can sometimes make defining what is and is not a parable challenging. To illustrate the point, here are a few examples that qualify as Hebrew parables.

Metaphor, figurative speech—John 10:7, 11; 15:1
Proverb—1 Samuel 24:13; Luke 4:23

Riddle[1]—Ezekiel 17:2; Habakkuk 2:6

Allegory and narrative parables—2 Samuel 2:11–20; Ezekiel 24:2–5; Matthew 21:28; 22:2-14; Luke 16:1; 8:2

Simile[2]—Matthew 17:20; Mark 4:30–32

Visual parables—the child used to illustrate the greatest in the Kingdom, Matthew 18:2; the cursing of the fig tree, Mark 11:13–21; the washing of the disciples' feet, John 13:3–5, 15.

Therefore, to limit the Hebrew or Aramaic parables to the narrower Greek definition is, as Jeremias put it, "to impose upon them an alien law." By merging this mixture of categories into what defines a parable, we can expand our perception, allowing us to listen more acutely with a first-century Jewish ear.

Why Did Jesus Teach through Parables?

1. Jesus's primary purpose in telling parables was to make disciples. He also spoke to them to enlighten those closest to him about the secrets of the Kingdom's nature. They cast new light on once-hidden characteristics of the Reign of God.
2. Parables like the Parable of the Good Samaritan were used to disarm his antagonists. Parables allow an opponent to examine himself and force him to lay down his offensive.
3. The parables also reveal the nature of God. For example, knowing God intimately is shown in the Parable of the Lost Son. The father of the lost son is seen setting aside the dignities of a village patriarch by running to his disgraced son to embrace and receive him again—something that would have raised eyebrows in an ancient Jewish village. This father willingly disgraced himself to save his son from humiliation at home. This parable shocked Jesus' audience when they associated God with a loving father willing to humiliate himself to receive a wayward son.
4. Parables have a way of demanding a response from the listener, as in the Parable of the Merciful King, where the listener is encouraged to forgive from the heart.
5. It was prophesied that the Messiah would teach in parables. Matthew paraphrases Asaph, who wrote, "I will open my mouth in parables. I

will utter things hidden since the creation of the world." Without the help of the Holy Spirit, there is no indication that this is Messianic. The author used an Old Testament passage in a way that was familiar to Jews of the first century. Matthew's inspired paraphrase of this passage is applied to Christ as a teacher of parables.

6. The Shema contains two great commandments upon which the Law and the Prophets were hung. The Jews considered the purpose of parables to be the interpretation of the Torah. The Jews believed that until Solomon, no one could correctly interpret the Torah. The rabbis considered him to be the first in Israel to teach through the use of parables. We call them *Proverbs*. Craig Evans makes an interesting observation along these lines. He points out the parallel between Solomon (a son of David, a speaker of parables, and an interpreter of the Torah) and Jesus (*the* Son of David, a speaker of parables, and an interpreter of the Torah). Were the Jews expecting a second Solomon who would interpret the Torah through parables? The answer is, perhaps. Jesus did not speak in parables merely because it was expected of a Jewish rabbi but more likely because it was a Solomon-like feature of a first-century Messianic expectation. When Jesus said that "a greater than Solomon is here," he associated himself with Solomon, a master of parables, and claimed something greater than Solomon.

Therefore, Jesus' use of parables was more than a cultural formality or Messianic expectation. It was his way of interpreting the heart of the Torah for his disciples to stir the kingdom person to be like God. Parables also effectively enabled him to deal with his enemies. Finally, the use of Hebrew parables combined the brilliance of storytelling with the wisdom of God to create these highly condensed, power-packed points on the Reign of God. We have come to know them as the Parables of the Kingdom.

Food for Thought

1. The Jews believed the Law was given to Moses in two forms. What are these two forms?

2. Discuss the difference between *Torah* and *Law* from our Western perspective.

3. Jesus was educated in everything that was Jewish in his day. Discuss what he would have learned as a boy from the synagogue school.

4. The rabbis taught in parables. How are Jesus' parables similar in style to the parables of the rabbis? How are they different?

5. What does Westermann say is the primary function of a comparison in parables?

6. What is the difference between the Greek form of a parable and the Hebrew form?

7. List the reasons why Jesus taught in parables.

8. Discuss Evans's comparison of Jesus with Solomon and what Jesus said of himself compared to Solomon.

9. What is the most meaningful thing you learned from this lesson?

Chapter 2

Approaching the Sacred Text: A First-Century Jewish Hermeneutic

If this subject bores you, just skip to chapter three. It is challenging to summarize this topic adequately as it is widespread and complicated. Yet, it is a topic that needs to be considered in this study. By familiarizing ourselves as much as possible with how the first-century Jews read, interpreted, and taught from the sacred Scriptures, we can appreciate the Jewish approach to the Kingdom Parables of Jesus. This does not suggest that the first-century Jewish interpretation of Scripture was correct. Still, we need a frame of reference to approach the Kingdom Parables.

Before the days of Ezra, there was no need for a systematic method of interpreting Scripture. The prophets and priests served as depositories and interpreters of God's word for his people. However, by the first century A.D., the Jewish method of interpreting and studying the Hebrew Scriptures had developed into a well-defined and complex system that became increasingly complex over time.

The Problem with Jewish Interpretation

Joseph Shulam, a Hebrew scholar in Jerusalem, makes a good point on how difficult it is to state a specific set of rules. He writes, "Rabbinic literature provides us with different lists of such principles [of interpretation] . . . but none of the lists give a complete description of all the interpretive rules found in all forms of midrash."[3] Once again,

Midrash is Jewish commentary. Everett Ferguson gives the following points as a summary of the ancient Jewish approach to the sacred text. He writes that Jewish exegesis (the science of interpreting scripture) can be classified in the apostolic period under four headings (Ferguson 431):

(1) Literalist—the plain, straightforward meaning, though the rabbis often applied this in a hyper-literal way.
(2) Allegorical—an eternal spiritual meaning ... divorced from its historical setting.
(3) Pesher (suggests *"this is that"*)—the hidden mystery in a text clarified by its fulfillment.
(4) Midrashic—combining scriptures so as to give a new interpretation and applying it to new situations based on personal experience or some event.

Interestingly, the writers of the New Testament applied all four interpretive methods outlined by Ferguson. Keep in mind that all of the apostles were Jewish. All but one of the writers of the New Testament was from Hebrew stock, assuming the writer of the Book of Hebrews was likewise Jewish. Contrary to what some might think, these inspired men did not cease being Jewish when they came to Christ. In other words, when they embraced the new covenant of Christ, they continued to identify themselves very much with Israel. Having the same background as Jesus for the most part, the Holy Spirit integrated the same method of interpreting Scripture that was common in the late Second Temple period in their teachings. Ferguson illustrates this from the teachings of the apostles Paul and Matthew. Paul used the literalist approach when he said Christ is the "seed" in Galatians 3:16, but he used allegory when contrasting Hagar and Sarah in Galatians 4:21–31. Matthew revealed hidden mysteries that were fulfilled in Christ, characteristic of the Hebrew style of pesher. Paul also used this style when writing 1 Corinthians 15:54–55 to reveal the secrets of the bodily resurrection. Paul's use of the Old Testament is midrashic because he paraphrases Old Testament passages to apply to a present situation. You will notice this from his sermon in Acts 13. While the grammatical-historical rule, which states that a passage of Scripture must be understood exactly as the original speaker or writer intended and that it must be interpreted to have only one meaning, is perhaps the best rule for us to follow, it was not always applied in ancient Jewish or apostolic hermeneutics. But let's remember that the Holy Spirit inspired Paul. So, this is not arbitrary. It is intentional.

Another example is the way prophecy was used. The Jews understood that specific predictions were to be fulfilled. However, the Jews mostly looked for parallels and even multiple fulfillments. Regarding this Jewish method of handling the Old Testament, Neal Pryor, in his contribution to the book *Biblical Interpretation: Principles and Practice*, comments on this in the chapter *The Use of the Old Testament in the New*. Pryor writes:

> The relationship between the two testaments is not as simple as might seem at first, especially in the way New Testament writers make use of passages from the Old. The problems fall into two general categories. First, some Old Testament passages that are applied to the New Testament situations do not seem in their original context to refer to the events of the Christian era. Second, the New Testament sometimes does not seem to quote the Old's text faithfully, sometimes even changing the reading to fit the purpose of the writer.
>
> Is there evidence of dishonesty in the New Testament writers? Do they take unallowable liberties with the text? How could the Jews be convinced that the Old Testament predicted New Testament events by inaccurate quotes or strained exegesis? Or, did the New Testament writers employ exegesis from the Old Testament that was accepted in their day?"[4]

The most logical supposition is contained in Pryor's last question. *"Or, did the New Testament writers employ exegesis from the Old Testament that was accepted in their day?"* Ferguson agrees, saying, "[w]hat may seem strange to the modern reader is often not so strange, or even is right at home, in the setting of first-century Jewish interpretation."[5] Therefore, it would not be unacceptable to assume that the Holy Spirit communicated through the writers of the Bible to the Jews of the first century in a way they would have viewed as traditional. To state it another way, in order to win the Jews, the Holy Spirit communicated in Jewish ways.

Myriads of Interpretations

While the rabbis disagreed on many of the rules (the schools of Hillel and Shammai, to name a couple), they agreed upon several points. For instance, they viewed Scripture as the only path to Wisdom and Paradise and sought to interpret Scripture to that end. Several decades after Christ, they developed an acronym spelling the Aramaic word for Paradise (PRDS) that outlined four levels of study.

1. Every text had its simple meaning (called *peshat* in Hebrew).
2. Every text hinted at additional insights (called *remez* in Hebrew).
3. Every text included homilies, moral lessons, advice for proper living, and inspiration (called *derash* in Hebrew).
4. Every text revealed deeper meanings accessible to the trained reader (called *sod*).[6]

The rabbis believed that "plumbing all these levels, by exploring and comprehending all the nuances of meaning of even one biblical verse, a person entered paradise" (Stern 14). They believed each sentence contained "myriads of information. Peel back one layer of meaning, and another emerged—and beneath that, another and another" (Stern 14). They taught that each "verse in Torah yields seventy different interpretations" (Wylen 63). In short, it was believed that if a person could discover the unsearchable riches of the wisdom of God, paradise was assured. However, this rabbinic approach to Scripture prompted a rebuke from Jesus, which is recorded in John 5:39. "You diligently study the Scriptures because you think that by them you possess eternal life. These are the Scriptures that testify about me."

There is one point the rabbis agreed upon, and I believe it is central to our study. Just as each Scripture and its interpretation was intended to reveal or shed light upon the meaning of the Torah, the rabbinic parables of the late Second Temple period were intended to explain the Torah in terms of everyday life. One rabbinic midrash reads:

Through the parables of Solomon we master the words of the Torah. Our rabbis say: "Let the parable be lightly esteemed in your eyes, since by means of the parable a man can master the words of the Torah."[7]

We might disagree with the rabbis who believed that until Solomon arose, no one could properly understand the words of the Torah. However, the significance that the rabbis placed upon the purpose of Solomon's *parables* is worth noting. Parables were used to interpret the Torah.

The Shema and the Kingdom Parables

What is known as the *Shema*, which was highlighted in first-century worship, may not always be emphasized in our worship today—I regret to say. In first-century Jewish thought, the *Shema* was believed to be *where the Reign of God begins for the people of God* (*Shema* means "hear" or "obey"). Jesus and the rabbis called the Great Commandment *Shema* (cf. Mark 12:28ff.). *Shema* means "Hear!" It is comprised of three passages of Scripture: Deut. 6:4–9, 11:13–21, and Num. 15:37–41. Jesus quoted it. *"Hear, O Israel, the LORD our God, the LORD is one. And you shall love the LORD your God with all your heart and with all your soul and with all your mind and with all your strength"* (Mark 12:29–30)

According to the rabbis, reciting the *Shema* was linked to a personal acceptance of God's reign. Young writes, "The implicit acceptance of God's unity as well as unconditional surrender of mind and heart to his holy will which the love of God expressed in the 'Shema' implies, this is what is understood by the receiving of the Kingdom of God" (Young 284). This is very significant. It tells us that the *Shema* was understood as the foundation of God's reign in the worshiper's life. If parables were thought to explain the Torah, the *Shema* is the foundation of the Torah, then the Kingdom Parables and the *Shema* are inseparable.

Applying the Study of the Parables

How can all of this enhance our study of the parables of Jesus? It enhances it in four ways.
1. Jesus will be expected to teach like a Jewish rabbi.
2. I am convinced that the parables of Jesus were intended to function in the same way as other rabbinic parables of his day. Parables helped

to shed light upon the Torah, the nature of God, his sovereign rule, his righteousness, his grace, and truth through the everyday experiences of first-century Jewish life. These topics were not new concepts to Israel. We are mistaken to think that the grace of God is limited to the New Testament. Each of these truths is introduced and can be studied from the first five books of Moses.
3. While it might be surprising to learn that Jesus did not reveal anything new from his parables that had not already been shown in the Torah, his Messianic identity was new.
4. Jesus was expected to highlight the *Shema* as the basis for where the Reign of God begins in the disciple. He was heard illustrating the love mandate in parabolic ways, indicating the character of the King and his reign. By drawing his listeners' attention to the Shema, the listener was drawn to him and made a disciple to be justified by faith in Jesus, their Messiah. All of this makes the statement about Jesus that is recorded in Mark 1:22 much more meaningful. "The people were amazed at his teaching because *he taught them as one who had authority, not as the teachers of the law*" (emphasis mine).

Food for Thought

1. When did the development of biblical interpretation (hermeneutics) become a study system for the word of God?

2. Discuss the apostles' method of interpretation, which was consistent with the first-century Jewish use of Scripture.

3. What problems arise from the first-century Jewish method of interpretation?

4. Discuss the rabbinic opinion about Solomon's use of parables in relation to the Torah.

5. What is the *Shema*?

6. What significance did the Jews place upon the recital of the *Shema*?

7. List the four ways that the study of the Jewish methods of interpretation of Scripture enhances our study of the parables of Jesus.

8. What is the most meaningful thing you learned from this lesson?

Chapter 3

The Jewish Concept of the Kingdom of God

The Kingdom Parables of Jesus deal with the nature of God and his Lordship, most often referred to as the Reign of God, the Kingdom of God, or the Kingdom of Heaven. Because there is some confusion about the Kingdom of God today, examining the Kingdom's nature in two areas is needed before we study the Kingdom Parables. In this chapter, we will consider the following:
1. The Jewish interpretation of the Kingdom of God during the late Second Temple period.
2. The Jewish expectation of the coming Kingdom and the Messiah.

The Jewish Perception of the Kingdom of God

In his Kingdom Parables, Jesus affirms or corrects Jewish perceptions of the Kingdom of God. The first Jewish perception of the Kingdom, which Jesus will affirm, is that the Kingdom of God and the Kingdom of Heaven are the same. To the Jews of Jesus' day, the mere mention of either term brought to mind Scriptures such as "The LORD reigns forever and ever" (Exodus 15:18). They understood the concept of the Kingdom as conveying a combination of ideas.
1. The *Shema* affirms God's oneness (*"Hear, O Israel: The LORD our God, the LORD is one"*). Again, accepting God's reign begins with the Shema's acceptance.
2. Divine protection.
3. Deliverance from bondage and the oppression of their enemies.
4. The demand for obedience to his commandments.
5. Forgiveness of sins—both personal and national.

6. They associated the final judgment and a new creation with the Kingdom of God.

This last point developed early during the apocalyptic movement of the Second Temple period. George R. Beasley-Murray writes that, with Isaiah 65–66 as a precedent for the apocalyptic works of Jewish literature, "It was inevitable that an increased emphasis on the transcendent features of the future Kingdom would lead to an expectation that *the coming of God will issue in a judgment of all generations of mankind, and a kingdom of God in a transformed creation*" (emphasis mine; Beasley-Murray 47)

To summarize the Jewish perception of the Kingdom of God, the basic theme as the Jews imagined it focused on God's reign, his overruling control, future blessings as the nation, and God's control over their present circumstances. These insights will be affirmations that Jesus will make in his parables.

Their ideal description of the Kingdom was nationalistic and political. This can be seen simply by examining the disciples Jesus chose and the people surrounding him. One of the disciples was a Zealot (Matt. 10:4). The Zebedee brothers requested seats of authority in the Kingdom (Matt. 20:20–21). The multitude sought to make Jesus their king to overthrow King Herod and Roman oppression (John 6:15). In Luke 24, the two disciples on the road to Emmaus lamented that Jesus did not redeem Israel. They envisioned the reinstatement of Israel's people to their original lands, the rebuilding of Solomon's Temple, the forgiveness of Israel's sins, and the inauguration of the Davidic King as their Messiah who would rule Jerusalem forever. These will be ideas of the Kingdom that Jesus corrected.

Messianic Hope

You may be surprised by this detail. According to rabbinic teachings, the Messiah was *not* expected to usher in the new world order of God's rule. It was the reverse. The Coming One was only expected to be a part of the advent of the Kingdom rather than the decisive factor (Ferguson 438). Beasley-Murray points out that "the function that Jesus assigns to himself in relation to the Kingdom goes well beyond anything said of the

Messiah in the Old Testament or the apocalyptic and rabbinic teaching of his day" (146). Wylen states that "the doctrine of Christ [as the New Testament teaches it] does not exist anywhere in first-century Judaism" (172). It seems that their dreams of the Kingdom were more about the nation and the age to come than the coming of the Messiah. He was only expected to be part of the blessings. Still, to say that the importance of the coming of the Messiah in Jewish expectations was minimal would be a serious misrepresentation. There is no doubt that the Jewish people looked for a Messiah, but the "Messianic hope" (as our generation has coined the phrase) is merely a part of the bigger picture. With eyes upon the horizon and looking for the arrival of the Kingdom of God, they also awaited the appearance of one other figure. Jewish tradition interpreted Micah 2:13 as speaking of two main characters with the Kingdom's arrival. It was the return of Elijah.

> The one who breaks open the way will go up before them; they will break through the gate and go out. Their king will pass through before them, the LORD at their head.

The "one who breaks open the way" is interpreted as Elijah of Malachi 3:1, allowing the King, the Messiah, to pass. The people of Judea expressed this eager anticipation in the days of John the Baptizer. They incorrectly believed that John was the Messiah (Luke 3:15), while some thought Jesus was Elijah, the forerunner of the Messiah (Matt. 16:14). To suspect either one to be Elijah meant they looked for the Messiah nearby in time. Jesus settled their speculations by stating publicly that John had come in the spirit of Elijah, leaving himself to be identified as the Messiah (Matt. 11:14).

Jewish notions of what the Messiah would be like were diverse. Still, a few common Messianic characteristics were shared among the Jews during the late Second Temple period, reflecting the Old Testament's allusions, predictions, and apocalyptic prophecies. Although these mainly focused on the Reign of God in the age to come, they correctly looked for a Messiah from the royal line of David. Their mistake was to expect a political leader to overthrow Roman rule and establish Israel as the dominant power (Oesterley 46).

Another common expectation of the Messiah was that he would be the *Second Moses*. The acts of the Messiah were expected to resemble the Exodus and the miracles of Moses. The literary composition of the Gospel of John does bear this out.[8] As we have already mentioned, they also expected a Solomon-like Messiah. Other less popular expectations of the Messiah include that of the Essenes of the Qumran community, who expected two Messiahs—one from the tribe of Judah who would serve as King of Israel and a second priestly Messiah from the tribe of Levi and a descendant of Aaron. On the other side of the aisle were the Sadducees and priests who did not expect a Messianic figure to arrive (Young 60). None of these expectations accounted for the Messiah to come in the way he did and be crucified on a Roman cross.

When considering the most commonly shared features outlined by the rabbis in some chronological order, the events of the coming new age were believed to work like this. The new era would begin with the coming of God and the Day of the LORD when the enemies of God would be overthrown. At that time, the Kingdom of God would be established in Jerusalem, ushering in Elijah and the days of the Messiah. Ferguson writes that the "days of the Messiah" varied according to Jewish writings (Ferguson 438). Some said it would be forty years (b Sanhedrin 99a). Another source said it would last four hundred years (2 Esdras 7:28–29; *Pesikta Rabbati* 4a). Yet another source has the "days of the Messiah" lasting for 1,000 years (*Midrash* on Psalms 90:17). At the end of the "days of the Messiah," some apocalyptic writings predicted the judgment of all generations and the Reign of God being set up in a literal new heaven and a new earth.

In Jewish thought, the Messiah wasn't expected to bring the Kingdom. This might surprise some, as we tend to view Christ and his predictions from a different point of view. The challenge for us—on this side of the empty tomb—is to read the first-century Jewish expectations of the Kingdom without our Christological lenses. We can indeed see things more clearly from the vantage point Jesus has provided us. Still, we must remember that it is a vantage point the Jews of the first half of the late Second Temple period did not have.

So, what do we gain from all of this? Despite being mixed with speculation and imagination, many Jewish expectations of the coming kingdom with the new age were close to being on track. The prevailing hypothesis was that the age to come would be a time of regeneration and restoration under the protection of the Messiah. At least in concept, their expectations were very accurate. If we take this as a place to begin, there was enough richness in Jewish soil for Jesus to sow the seed of the Kingdom and expect a harvest.

Food for Thought

1. Discuss the six ideas associated with the Kingdom of God from the first-century Jewish perspective.

2. What concepts of the Kingdom in the first century did Jesus correct?

3. Define the Messianic hope from the first-century Jewish point of view.

4. When considering the most common features of the Kingdom outlined by the rabbis in chronological order, what element may surprise us?

5. What is the most meaningful thing you learned from this lesson?

Chapter 4

The Reign of God in the Old Testament

The Kingdom Parables are about the Kingdom of Heaven or the Kingdom of God. For this reason, we need to take this chapter and focus on the Kingdom. The first-century Jewish concept of the Kingdom of God was limited to what had been revealed by Moses and the prophets, mixed with apocalyptic visions and assorted expectations. They took these and pieced together a mosaic of a complex end-of-times belief system from this mix. This chapter examines the Kingdom of God from Moses to the prophets. Jesus may have spoken from the backdrop of the Jewish perspective of the Kingdom (when these perceptions were correct), but he based his teachings of the Kingdom of God on the Hebrew Scriptures. The Kingdom Parables will reflect what was already known from Scripture.

Kingdom or Reign?

The English terms "kingdom" and "reign" have clear and distinct meanings. However, in Hebrew, Aramaic, and Greek, they can be more ambiguous and context-dependent. Put simply, these words lack the fixed definitions that their English counterpart possess. This ambiguity deserves our attention and study of how these words were treated at the time of Christ. How does the Bible use the concept of the Kingdom? Do the original words refer to God's rule or a specific domain? Do they describe God's current activities or events yet to unfold?

Let's begin with something from Everett Ferguson. He writes that the Hebrew, Aramaic, and Greek words for *kingdom* refer more to reign and not realm, to dominion and not domain (Ferguson, *The Church of*

Christ, 19). Our English word *kingdom* does not automatically communicate what it once did in the seventeenth century when King James I of England authorized a new translation of the Bible. Mortimer Arias says, "Our generation has a problem with the very concept of kingdom in a time of democracies and democratic ideologies" (Arias 41). This has contributed to an institutionalized concept of the Kingdom. As a consequence, misleading doctrinal positions have been established on the sole proposition that the Kingdom of God is defined as a domain with a king, territory, law, and subjects. This is why we adjust our understanding by studying the unique use of the Hebrew, Aramaic, and Greek words as they were used during the late Second Temple period and as Jesus used them.

The Kingdom in the Old Testament

The Old Testament does not use the phrases Kingdom of God and Kingdom of Heaven, but it does contain many references to the Kingdom of God. The nation of Israel did not doubt who ruled as King of kings, even when they were rejecting him. Here are just a few examples from the Old Testament that speak of the extent of God's reign. The emphasis in the following verses is mine.

- Exodus 15:18—"The LORD will **reign** forever and ever."
- 1 Chronicles 16:30–31—Tremble before him, all the earth! The world is firmly established; it cannot be moved. Let the heavens rejoice, let the earth be glad; let them say among the nations, "The LORD **reigns**!"
- Psalm 9:5–7—You have rebuked the nations and destroyed the wicked; you have blotted out their name forever and ever. Endless ruin has overtaken the enemy; you have uprooted their cities; even the memory of them has perished. The LORD **reigns** forever; he has established his throne for judgment.
- Psalm 29:10—The LORD sits enthroned over the flood; the LORD is enthroned as **King** forever.
- Psalm 47:7–9—For God is the **King** of all the earth; sing to him a psalm of praise. God **reigns** over the nations; God is seated on his holy throne. The nobles of the nations assemble as the people of

the God of Abraham, for the kings of the earth belong to God; he is greatly exalted.
- Psalm 93:1–2—The LORD **reigns**, he is robed in majesty; the LORD is robed in majesty and is armed with strength. The world is firmly established; it cannot be moved. Your throne was established long ago; you are from all eternity.
- Psalm 99:1–2—The LORD **reigns**, let the nations tremble; he sits enthroned between the cherubim, let the earth shake. Great is the LORD in Zion; he is exalted over all the nations.
- Psalm 103:19—The LORD has established his throne in heaven, and his **kingdom** rules over all.
- Psalm 113:4–6—The LORD is exalted over all the nations, his glory above the heavens. Who is like the LORD our God, the One who sits enthroned on high, who stoops down to look on the heavens and the earth?
- Psalm 145:13—Your **kingdom** is an everlasting **kingdom**, and your dominion endures through all generations. The LORD is faithful to all his promises and loving toward all he has made.
- Isaiah 40:22—He sits enthroned above the circle of the earth, and its people are like grasshoppers. He stretches out the heavens like a canopy, and spreads them out like a tent to live in.
- Lamentations 5:19—You, O LORD, reign forever; your throne endures from generation to generation.
- Psalm 103:19—***"His kingdom rules over all."*** Throughout the Old Testament, it is emphatically stated that the Kingdom of God is all-encompassing and eternal. In addition to these affirmations, other Psalms of David declare the glory of the Kingdom of God as being "forever and ever." The prophet Isaiah saw the eternal King high and lifted up and seated on his throne (6:1–5). Jeremiah testified, "The LORD is the true God; He is the living God, the eternal King" (Jer. 10:10). The ***domain*** of Nebuchadnezzar, a Babylonian pagan king, was taken from him because the ***dominion*** belonged to the Most High. This caused Nebuchadnezzar to confess the supreme sovereignty of the God of the Jews (Dan. 4:17) and the *ever-present activity* of God's rule.

His reign possesses the same attributes and qualities as all that emanates from his Being. As a result, his reign expresses his character, glory, and power. Just as his spoken word is living and powerful (Heb. 4:12) and does not return to him empty but achieves the purpose for which he sends it (Isa. 55:11), the Reign of God is living and powerful, serving his purposes over all things created.

With this understanding, even the spider making its web in the corner of the room is within the Kingdom of God. A sparrow cannot fall without his notice. Everything visible and invisible, animate and inanimate, living and dead, good and evil, is in his kingdom because it is within his dominion and domain.

The Realm of God

Understanding his reign in these terms helps to broaden our understanding of the secondary use of the word *kingdom* as it relates to *God's realm*. God's realm becomes representative of his reign, sharing an identity with him, and becomes a calling, as seen first in Israel and finally in the church. Israel, under the first covenant, was representative of God's reign over the nations of the earth in those days. As the realm of God, the nation of Israel was his "kingdom of priests" and a "holy nation" (Exo. 19:6)). Similarly, the church of Christ, which is the full expectation of Israel under the new and final covenant, is representative of God's reign on the earth today. Therefore, the church is called the "kingdom" (Matt. 16:18–19; Col. 1:13; Rev. 1:6), "a royal priesthood" (1 Peter 2:9), and a "holy nation" of God.

God's realm is also identified by where he places his name. God said to David regarding Solomon, "He is the one who will build a house for my Name, and I will establish the throne of his kingdom forever." Within this prediction were the Messianic implications of God's reign and realm while identifying where his name would be placed. In Ephesians 3:14-17, Paul, the apostle, prayed with God's reign and realm in mind, recognizing the "name" given to the family of God, and identified the dwelling place of Christ. He wrote, "For this reason, I kneel before the Father, from whom his whole family in heaven and on earth derives its name. I pray that out of his glorious riches, he may strengthen you with power through his Spirit in your inner being, so that Christ may dwell in your hearts through faith." God identified the realm of his dwelling from the Temple of Solomon and the people of Israel under the old covenant while ruling over the nations. Today, God identifies his realm as being the temple of the Christian's heart and the global family of God under the new covenant while ruling over the nations. The *realm* of God has always been identified by where he places his name, while his *reign* remains universal, as it has always been.

The Multidimensional Kingdom of God

Earlier, I mentioned how everything visible and invisible, animate and inanimate, living and dead, good and evil, is in God's kingdom. That's quite a statement. I agree. But once we correctly understand the Kingdom from the Hebrew Scriptures by distinguishing the terms *reign* and *realm*, we open up the sovereignty of God in its broader sense. This broader sense demonstrates what Arias calls a multidimensional quality of the Kingdom of God (Arias xv). Jesus and the writers of the New Testament agree with and further reveal this multidimensional nature of the Kingdom alluded to in the Old Testament. Here is a sampling. Again, the emphasis in each of the following verses is mine:

- Luke 17:20–21—*"Once, having been asked by the Pharisees when the Kingdom of God would come, Jesus replied, 'The Kingdom of God does not come with your careful observation, nor will people say, 'Here it is,' or 'There it is,' because the **Kingdom of God is within you**."* Jesus highlights a dimension of God's rule emphasizing internal activity (McGuiggan 64).
- Matthew 12:28—*"But if I drive out demons by the Spirit of God, then **the Kingdom of God has come upon you**."* This verse shows an outward demonstration of the Reign of God in the presence of Jesus and eyewitnesses.
- Luke 21:31—*"Even so, when you see these things happening, you know that **the Kingdom of God is near**."* The context is the prophecy of the A.D. 70 destruction of Jerusalem. The nearness of the Kingdom of God here is apparent by his rule over the advancing Roman armies upon Jerusalem. The Roman war machine was a demonstration of the enthroned Messiah's reign.
- Matthew 16:18–19—*"And I tell you that you are Peter, and on this rock I will build **my church**, and the gates of Hades will not overcome*

*it. I will give you the **keys of the Kingdom of heaven**; whatever you bind on earth will be bound in heaven, and whatever you loose on earth will be loosed in heaven."* The words *kingdom* and *church* are used interchangeably, describing a present dimension or spiritual realm of the redeemed in Christ. Paul identifies those in this dimension as seated with Christ in the heavenly realms (cf. Eph. 2:6).

- Colossians 1:13—*"For he has rescued us from the dominion of darkness and brought us into **the Kingdom of the Son** he loves."* Paul says we have been delivered from the power of darkness and translated into the Kingdom of the Son. In verse eighteen, Jesus is shown to be the head of the body, the church. Again, the Kingdom and the church can be considered inseparable in their proper context where Christians are spoken of as being delivered from one realm into another, i.e., from Satan's to Christ's domain.

From this text, another very important observation can be established. Though inseparable from the Kingdom of God, the church of Christ does not compose or define God's entire rule. Notice the five dimensions that must be included in the reign of Christ from Colossians 1:13–19.

1. Christ rules over the material universe.
2. Christ rules over the spiritual realm.
3. Christ rules over all nations of the world.
4. Christ rules over wicked people, those without hope, and without God in the world (Ephesians 2:12).
5. Christ rules over his people, the redeemed, both living on earth and with him in Paradise.

Naturally, his righteous ones are at the heart of the Reign of God. He rules them with a scepter of righteousness (Heb. 1:8). Everyone else is ruled by a rod of iron (cf. Psalm 2:9; 145:11–13; Rev. 2:27.), whether they want to be or not. Jim McGuiggan makes a very good point, which should be added here.

> To say the Kingdom is "spiritual" is correct. But if by saying this we mean it is confined to religious goings on within the Christian, we are badly off the mark. **Christ is King over more than the hearts of Christians!** His sovereignty is not to be cramped within buildings with stained glass windows. To make

the point that God aims to reign within every heart is biblical. To say he rules nowhere and nothing else is false! It is easier to fall into this error when we narrow the "kingdom of God" down until it is co-existent with the "Church." These two are **not** to be regarded as identical! (McGuiggan 65).

This multidimensional picture perfectly fits the Old Testament's view of the Reign or Kingdom of God. The only thing we find new or added to it concerns the reigning authority delegated to God's Son, Jesus, the enthroned Messiah (Matt. 28:18). On this aspect of his authority, Paul says Jesus must reign until he has handed the Kingdom back to his Father when all his enemies are conquered (1 Cor. 15:24–26). Until then, he reigns as King of kings and Lord of lords. The Son of David is the Sovereign One.

The Kingdom of God is a multifaceted and all-encompassing reality, extending beyond the confines of the church. In Scripture, it is depicted as God's dynamic and authoritative rule over the visible and invisible domains, whether characterized by righteousness or wickedness, life or death. Depending on the context, the Kingdom might pertain exclusively to the redeemed, representing either the remnant of Israel or the body of believers in Christ. Additionally, the Kingdom of God can encompass the entirety of creation. This includes the dimension of time itself. The Reign of God can be ambiguously described as simultaneously existing in the past, present, future, or all of these. Alternatively, the Kingdom may denote a particular manifestation of God's power observed at a specific moment in time, such as when Jesus bestowed sight upon the blind, exorcised demons, or mobilized a Gentile army for a divine purpose. The Reign of God might also symbolize a future glory to anticipate.

When we grasp the comprehensive nature of the Kingdom of God, with its various dimensions, we gain insight into the extent of God's sovereignty. This biblical model enables us to place unwavering trust in him. Ultimately, this is God's desired outcome for humanity. His sovereignty serves as the unshakable foundation on which we trust Jesus, the Messiah. His power embodies his rule, manifesting as salvation and judgment. This is the concept of the Kingdom illustrated in Jesus' parables.

Food for Thought

1. Discuss the differences between the English words *kingdom* and *reign*.

2. Discuss what Ferguson and Arias say about the word *kingdom* and how our common use of the word has shaped the narrow way we interpret the Kingdom of God.

3. Discuss the Reign of God as revealed in the Old Testament. Consider the scope, sphere, and results of his reign.

4. Describe how the Reign of God is distinguished from Nebuchadnezzar's rule in Daniel chapter 4.

5. Discuss the two purposes for the *realm* of God as a Kingdom and how these are identified in the Old and New Testaments.

6. What does Arias mean when he says that the Kingdom of God is *multi-dimensional?*

7. Discuss how the Kingdom of God is revealed as multidimensional from the New Testament.

8. McGuiggan states, "To say the Kingdom is 'spiritual' is correct. But if by saying this we mean it is confined to religious goings-on within the Christian, we are badly off the mark." Why does he say this?

9. How does the Kingdom concept outlined in this chapter affect your concept of the Kingdom of God?

10. What is the most meaningful thing you learned from this lesson?

Chapter 5

Guidelines for Explaining the Parables

One of my teachers rightly said that parables have long been seedbeds for error, speculation, and private interpretation. This makes the setting of guidelines and the establishing of boundaries imperative so that errors of the past can be avoided. However, caution still needs to be exercised. The parables are unique from other genres in the Bible. As Kenneth Bailey advises: "any attempt to state in propositional terms a tightly constructed interlocking system of interpretative principles, which can be applied uniformly to all the parables of Jesus, is doomed to failure" (Bailey 38). Forcing tightly constructed rules of interpretation on the parables will not do. This is why guidelines are suggested to help set reasonable margins. Otherwise, the sky is the limit when applying meaning to the details of Jesus' parables.

1. Avoid the temptation to over-allegorize the parables. W.O.E. Oesterley wrote, "A parable is explained, an allegory is interpreted" (63). Archibald Hunter defines an allegory as "the interpretation of a text in terms of something else, regardless of what that something else might be" (23). Someone else has defined an allegory simply as a series of metaphors strung together. Historically, allegorizing Scripture was popularized in the Second Temple period with Philo, an Alexandrian Jewish philosopher. He is regarded as instrumental in making the Greek allegory a part of ancient Judaism and is considered responsible for marrying the faith of Israel with Greek philosophy. Consequently, allegory became a standard part of Jewish interpretation of Scripture. The danger associated with allegorizing Scripture is that it is too subjective and exposes it to various interpretations. The ancient rabbis made thorough use of

allegory in their interpretations. It did not matter to them that their interpretations contradicted each other. Because of the allowances they gave themselves, each interpretation was considered correct. Jesus did use allegories to some degree and expected his disciples to understand what he taught correctly, but the Holy Spirit inspired him. There was a big difference.

2. Not every detail is intended to convey meaning. This should be added to our previous point on allegorizing parables. One who is considered the *maestro* in the art of allegorizing the parables of Jesus is a third-century A.D. Greek "Christian" philosopher by the name of Origen (Hunter 25). He mastered the art of allegorizing to the degree of becoming absurd by attaching ridiculous meaning to every minute detail. To arbitrarily apply meaning to details of a parable simply because it seems to fit is too subjective and unwarranted. The first-century Jewish listener would not have given such attention to the externals. Oesterley makes the point that "it was a fundamental principle of Jewish parabolic teaching that the external form of the parable was of relatively secondary importance; the purpose of a parable was that upon which attention was concentrated. It would never have entered the mind of one of the Lord's hearers to worry about the external form of a parable" (82). A good illustration of this is found in the Parable of the Hidden Treasure. The Jewish audience would have concentrated on the value of what the man found rather than his stumbling upon it and the question of his ethics by not informing the owner about the treasure.

3. Pay attention to things that are rooted in the Hebrew Scriptures. The Jews sought parallels, patterns, comparisons, and Messianic language to convey meaning. They would have asked questions like, does the parable contain familiar pictures, figures of speech, or metaphors that are automatically identified as possessing meaning? If a definition has already been applied to something, and the context does not suggest otherwise, why seek to reinterpret it?

4. Try to understand the primary truth of the parable without making the parable the primary truth. This is a point made by Jim McGuiggan.[9] The primary truth will be established either in the context or elsewhere in Scripture. The parable is designed to illustrate a particular aspect of the truth.

5. Do not take that which is intended to be figurative literally. This is another point taken from McGuiggan. It is not uncommon for parables to use imagery without an interpretation. Apocalyptic language should be viewed as figurative, as merely a part of the overall picture. It might or might not contribute to the interpretation.
6. Consider the context. Context plays a major role in properly explaining a parable. Within the context, there should be indicators that help apply meaning to the parable. Jesus never uttered a parable that was disconnected from the framework of his surroundings. The players or objects in the parable are very often symbols of things within the cultural backdrop, so the parables of Christ are not isolated. Context also determines their function. It makes the parable communicate better to the listener. Context reveals the cultural, religious, and political dynamics that govern a parable. The context prevents the parable from appearing just pulled out of the air.

Let Jesus explain his parables. If there is one ironclad rule, this is it. Jesus will, at times, interpret a parable either at the introduction, at the conclusion, or within the context. Good examples are the Parable of the Sower and the Parable of the Weeds in the Field. There is no better interpreter than Jesus. Look for Jesus' explanation before making any applications.

Food for Thought

1. Why does Kenneth Bailey advise against constructing an "interlocking system of interpretative principles, which can be applied uniformly to all the parables of Jesus"?

2. Discuss the problems associated with allegorizing parables.

3. How did a Jewish listener view a parable's external form or details?

4. What does McGuiggan say about the primary truth of a parable?

5. Discuss why the context of a parable is so important to interpreting the meaning of a parable.

6. What is the number one rule regarding parables?

7. What is the most meaningful thing you learned from this lesson?

Part 2

Chapter 6

Kingdom Parables in Jewish Soil

We needed to discuss the topics of the first five chapters before discussing the Kingdom Parables to lay a proper foundation. The Jewish soil from which these parables grow will become more and more appreciated as we study them with their Jewishness intact. This will give us a fresh reading of the Kingdom Parables from the vantage point of Jesus' original listeners: Jewish fishermen, farmers, and village peasants. We cannot rightly speak of the Kingdom of God without that Jewish connection. To ignore this fundamental distinction would be like trying to understand American history without considering the significance of Ellis Island. When the parables of Christ are projected through this ancient Jewish prism, the prophets of old, and a shared human experience, we are inspired toward God-like character as kingdom people.

Immediately noticeable in the Kingdom Parables are the following things:

1. They announced and illustrated the Messiah's reign. In them, Jesus is revealed as the Son of David, the King of Israel; the Son of God; the Son of Man; the Commander of the angels; the Judge of Israel and the world; the Sower of the sons of the Kingdom; and the owner of the Vineyard, Israel, and the Kingdom.
2. These parables affirmed the eternal destiny of Israel if they accepted Jesus as their Messiah. The eternal destiny for Israel was—and is— to be justified by faith in *Yeshua*. However, because they rejected God's Messiah and his reign, the parables served to warn Jerusalem

of the coming judgment as the prophets from Daniel to Malachi predicted it. Principally, however, Jesus came announcing through the parables that the Reign of God is here—now. C. H. Dodd writes that Jesus "[…] used parables to enforce and illustrate the idea that the Kingdom of God had come upon men there and then."[1] He adds, regarding the intervention of God through Jesus, that the parables of the Kingdom present the hour of decision for the Jewish people. Dodd calls it "realized eschatology" (159). This is just another way of saying that the Reign of God that will end all things has arrived, and Jesus will have the final word.

The Method of Our Study

The parables of Matthew 13, Mark 4, and Luke 8 are intended to introduce the Kingdom through parables. First, we will examine the context and setting of each parable, followed by an examination of their Jewish background. Once these areas are sufficiently discussed, we will turn to the audience to see how the parable challenged them. Finally, we will consider any appropriate applications for ourselves.

The Kingdom Parables recorded in this context are spoken during Jesus' first Galilean tour. The setting begins in Matthew 12:22 and Mark 3:20, with Jesus entering a house as a crowd gathers (presumably in Capernaum). A demon-possessed man, who was also blind and mute, was brought to Jesus and was healed. Exorcizing demons was not unusual. The disciples witnessed an unidentified man casting out demons in the name of Jesus and were told not to forbid him from doing so.[3] Jesus acknowledged that some of the Pharisees could cast out demons. Rather than dismissing their blasphemous accusations, he chided them, saying, "And if I drive out demons by Beelzebub, by whom do your people drive them out? So then, they will be your judges." Then, there is an account in Acts 19:13. Luke documented an exorcism by a group of Jews who traveled around exorcizing evil spirits. So, exorcism was not anything new.

However, there was no doubt about the uniqueness of Jesus' miracles. When the people witnessed the miracles of Jesus, they asked, *"Could this be the Son of David?"* The phrase *Son of David* had always been a royal title for the Messiah. But what was it that raised their Messianic inquiry? It was the miracle of restoring sight to the blind man. Giving sight to the blind was a miracle the Jews believed was reserved for the Messiah. No prophet in the Old Testament ever healed anyone of blindness. There were three major miracles the rabbis said could not be performed by a mere man and were considered Messianic miracles (Fruchtenbaum, 1–22).

- Healing of the lepers.
- Giving sight to the blind (Isa. 61:1–2).
- Healing the deaf and mute.

It was a common practice of the Sanhedrin to send a delegation to investigate serious messianic hopefuls. So, this gathering of curious skeptics was predictable. Self-proclaimed messiahs rose and recruited followers from time to time throughout the Second Temple period. Finding followers was not difficult in an age when the expectation of the Messiah was high. Gamaliel mentions two false messiahs in Acts 5:36–37 that had risen and fallen. Jesus was suspected of being just another one to be added to the list. This Messianic examination involved two stages (Fruchtenbaum 6): (1) *Stage of Observation*—A delegation from the Sanhedrin would observe whether any Messianic signs were being performed. (2) *Stage of Interrogation—the Pharisees and Sadducees thoroughly interrogated Jesus*. Their questions were mostly to see how orthodox he was to their traditions.

After Jesus cast out the demon and gave the man his sight and speech, the Pharisees quickly tried to discredit his miracle by calling it a demonstration of demonic power. They rejected the possibility of this being a demonstration of the presence of the Reign (Kingdom) of God. Restoring sight should have been sufficient testimony that Jesus *is* the Son of David, but they reacted with hostility and rejected the Messianic witness of his miracles. However, it was evident that the eyewitnesses in the crowd were formulating their own opinions without the aid of the Sanhedrin delegation. It was apparent that the Pharisees' control of the situation was being undermined.

Jesus' response to their blasphemy is the first illustration of the word *kingdom* being used to describe God's active reign, rule, or dominion, not realm or domain. He said, *"But if I drive out demons by the Spirit of*

*God, then **the Kingdom of God has come upon you***"(emphasis mine; Matt. 12:28; Luke reads, "If it is by the finger of God, "11:20). In other words, God demonstrated his rule over Satan at that moment. In that sense, the Kingdom of God was present, as they should have realized.

After insulting and sinning against the Holy Spirit by their satanic allegation, they went even further with their litmus test for messianic hopefuls by insisting from Jesus a miraculous sign. In other words, they were demanding something miraculously demonstrated in the heavens.[9] Jesus, frustrated by their evasiveness and blasphemy, made it clear that the miracle he had just performed would be as Messianic as his signs would be until his resurrection, as he referred to the sign of Jonah (Matt. 12:39–41.). This is when he condemned their evil, unbelieving hearts and warned of judgment against them with the parable of the unclean spirit (Matt. 12:42–45).

Jesus then addresses a less antagonistic group, although not all were believers. While Jesus was speaking to the crowd, his mother and brothers came to take him away.[12] But because it was so crowded, they could not approach him. I appreciate that God saw fit to include this testing of Mary's faith and the unbelief in Jesus' siblings in telling the story. All of us have moments of doubt and weakness. It helps us to see that Mary had something more in common with her fore-parents, Abraham and Sarah, who likewise wavered more than once in moments of apprehension and impatience. Jesus ignored his family's attempts to take him aside and announced that those who hear and practice God's word are his family. He was not rejecting his mother. Perhaps he was reminding her again of how he must be about his Father's business. Jesus did leave the house, but instead of going with them, he walked to the shoreline of the lake, where he entered a boat, enabling him to teach the crowd more effectively. It is here that we listen to him teach from nine parables.

The Key to Understanding the Parables

I am jumping ahead in the context for a moment to a proverb recorded in Mark 4:21–24 and Luke 8:16–18, in which Jesus speaks to his disciples. After telling the Parable of the Sower, Jesus revealed the secret to understanding the parables. Jesus said:

> No one lights a lamp and hides it in a jar or puts it under a bed. Instead, he puts it on a stand so that those who come in can see the light. For there is nothing hidden that will not be disclosed, and nothing concealed that will not be known or brought out into the open.

Naturally, the purpose of a lamp is to give light. However, before anyone can see the light, Jesus says they must *come in*. The idea seems that the closer a disciple is to Jesus, the clearer his understanding of the parable becomes, and consequently, the nature of the Reign of God. The *light* is not the parable but intended to draw the listener closer to Jesus, the true Light. Those drawn to him become his disciples, and as they give more of themselves in the process, they will receive more understanding about the Reign of God. He means, "With the same measure you use, it will be measured to you—and even more. Whoever has will be given more; whoever does not have, even what he has, will be taken from him," Jesus said. The key to understanding the parables of the Kingdom is discovered by becoming a disciple of Jesus.

Food for Thought

1. Discuss the context and setting of these parables. What happened that sparked controversy with the Pharisees?

2. What three miracles did the rabbis believe were reserved for the Messiah?

3. The Sanhedrin occasionally dealt with false messiahs. What are the two stages of investigation used by the delegation?

4. Discuss Jesus' use of the word *kingdom* in Matthew 12:28. How is it possible for the Kingdom to have come upon them at that moment?

5. Discuss Mary's momentary weakness in faith in her son and why she seems to be distracted. How would Jesus' brothers have played a role?

6. What statement by Jesus sets up the Parable of the Sower and the corresponding parables in the context?

7. Discuss the key to understanding the parables defined by Jesus in Mark 4:21–24 and Luke 8:16–18.

8. What is the most meaningful thing you learned from this lesson?

Chapter 7

The Parable of the Sower

Matthew 13:3–23; Mark 4:2–20; Luke 8:4–15

The context begins with a dramatic demonstration of the Reign—Kingdom—of God against the stronghold of Satan. Jesus cast out one of Satan's demons, who had kept a man blind and mute, by restoring his sight and speech. Confrontation resulted from the Pharisees who accused Jesus of working by the power of Satan and thereby insulting the Holy Spirit. With this as a backdrop, Jesus will illustrate five things from the following parables: (1) Why some believe and others do not; (2) How the Reign of God operates in the heart of the believer; (3) What the Reign of God is worth; (4) A warning of judgment when we refuse to hear and practice God's word; and (5) Jesus will promise vindication and redemption. The first parable is the Parable of the Sower. It is not introduced by the words, "The kingdom of heaven is like," but it serves as the seedbed for the following Kingdom Parables.

Matthew 13:3–9

"Then he told them many things in parables, saying: 'A farmer went out to sow his seed. As he was scattering the seed, some fell along the path, and the birds came and ate it up. Some fell on rocky places, where it did not have much soil. It sprang up quickly, because the soil was shallow. But when the sun came up, the plants were scorched, and they withered because they had no root. Other seed fell among thorns, which grew up and choked the plants. Still other seed fell on good soil, where it produced a crop—a hundred, sixty or thirty times what was sown.' He who has ears let him hear."

Jewish Background

This parable's geographical setting is in the vicinity of the Plain of Esdraelon in Galilee, which has some of the most fertile farmland in northern Israel and where the chief crops were wheat and barley. Wheat was sown in heavier rainfall areas, while barley was sown in small patches throughout the countryside. Barley was considered the poor man's wheat. A Palestinian peasant farmer would walk through a field scattering seeds with a seed bag draped over his shoulder. There were two harvest seasons. Sowing for the spring harvest was done between October and December. The second harvest came at the end of the growing season in the fall. The livelihood of the peasant farmer was dependent on the planting and harvesting cycle. Therefore, when Jesus spoke of sowing and harvesting, he touched on a very familiar experience.

Jesus said the seed was sown onto four soil types—pathway, rocky, among thorns, and good soil. Coming from a farming background in Kentucky, I can relate to this parable very well, although geographically, we are thousands of miles from where Jesus lived. In my home in Kentucky, we have red clay soil that can become very hard to handle. We have fields that seem to produce rocks with every plow turn. Gathering rocks from the field was an endless chore. We had fencerows overgrown with weeds, thistles, and sawbriers. Cleaning them in the summer served my father as a convenient means of discipline for three mischievous sons. We also had rich river-bottom and creek-bottom soil that produced yearly bumper crops.

A farmer knows the value of good soil. He also knows the expense of sowing. This parable describes a farmer sowing seed indiscriminately. His hand does not withhold seed from places he knows will not provide enough depth for the seed to take root or sprout, much less have a chance to mature. Those of us with a farming background might even question the wisdom of this man because it seems wasteful to sow seed in unprepared soil. Any listener with an agricultural background automatically knows which seed will do well and which will not, depending on the ground where it is sown. Nevertheless, the man in this parable scatters seed as if it were all good soil.

Application

Jesus does not interpret every parable, but he interprets this one. Matthew 13:18–23 gives the interpretation as follows:

> Listen then to what the parable of the sower means: When anyone hears the message about the Kingdom and does not understand it, the evil one comes and snatches away what was sown in his heart. This is the seed sown along the path. The one who received the seed that fell on rocky places is the man who hears the word and at once receives it with joy. But since he has no root, he lasts only a short time. He quickly falls away when trouble or persecution comes because of the word. The one who received the seed that fell among the thorns is the man who hears the word, but the worries of this life and the deceitfulness of wealth choke it, making it unfruitful. But the one who received the seed that fell on good soil is the man who hears the word and understands it. He produces a crop, yielding a hundred, sixty or thirty times what was sown.

A statement made by Jesus before leaving the house sets up the lesson of the Parable of the Sower. He said, "My mother and brothers hear God's word and put it into practice."[1] This statement gives purpose and meaning to the parable and demonstrates its truth. The audience represented the four soil types named in the parable. The pathway represents two groups: the accusation-making Sanhedrin delegation and the brothers of Jesus. John tells us that the brothers of Jesus were not believers at the time.[2] The soil described as the crowd represents rocky ground. They joyfully received the message of the Kingdom, but their faith will soon fade away. I have placed Mary, the mother of Jesus, in the category of thorny ground because, at that moment, her faith seems to be overshadowed by anxiety and cares created by her other sons, causing her faith to waver. She allowed herself to be persuaded by her unbelieving children to remove Jesus from the crowd, believing he was out of his mind.[3] Certainly, she was acting out of a mother's concern, but she was also being tested like everyone else by Jesus' words. The sword, predicted by old Simeon, was beginning to pierce her soul.[4] Mary demonstrates that—as a rule—the best of us will not go beyond the measure of our faith at any given moment. Anytime we allow doubt and worry to invade our thoughts, our faith is affected. Mary had great faith, as the New Testament shows us, but at this moment, she blinked.

The fourth group represented in this parable comprises the twelve disciples and the man healed by Jesus. They were nearest to Jesus at this point. They were in the crowd who had approached the illuminating Light to hear and comprehend his teachings. Again, as Jesus explained, the closer one is drawn to the lamp's light, the greater the opportunity to understand the mysteries of the Kingdom. Equally true, the greater the distance between Jesus and oneself, the more his teachings remain a mystery.

An Interesting Irony

This parable also presents an interesting irony. The context opens with Jesus demonstrating the power of the Reign of God over the reign of Satan. Yet the parable shows that as powerful as the Reign of God may demonstrate itself, Satan may snatch the seed (the message of the Reign of God) from the human heart. This seems to imply that the Reign of God in our lives is only as powerful as our faith will permit. We often think of power as something expressed by force. However, power could be expressed through restraint. At times, God chooses to withhold his hand from preventing Satan's thievery when we fail to respond appropriately due to our own apathy and indifference. For example, this is seen in Jesus' hometown. The Gospels document a visit Jesus made to Nazareth. It says, "He could not do any miracles there except lay his hands on a few sick people and heal them. And he was amazed at their lack of faith" (Matt. 13:54–58; Mark 6:1–6a.). His miraculous powers and wisdom—mentioned in Matthew 13:54—were evidence of the presence of God's reign. However, as the birds snatched the seed sown on the pathway, Satan was there to steal what Jesus sowed. The text says they were amazed at his wisdom and power, but amazement is not faith. Jesus was even more astonished at their disbelief. This is why there is an irony involved in this parable.

Therefore, the Reign of God possesses the power to prevent, protect, and provide in any given situation, but by his power, he may choose to exercise restraint. Whether it is permitting Satan to steal the message of the Kingdom from the hardened heart or defying Satan by casting out demons and producing righteousness one hundred times over, this ironic intervention is in his complete control because he rules over all things.

Food for Thought

1. Discuss the similarities and the differences between seed-sowing in Jesus' day and now.

2. Draw a parallel between the four types of soil and the four groups found in his audience.

3. Do you agree or disagree that Mary is found outside the circle of his immediate disciples at this moment? Discuss your opinion.

4. What is the irony of this parable and the event that prompted Jesus' response?

5. How does this parable relate to the nature of the Reign of God?

6. What is the most meaningful thing you learned from this lesson?

Chapter 8

The Parable of the Seed

Mark 4:26–29

On the farm, everything functions as a means to an end. What is done in the spring is with anticipation of the harvest in the fall. Likewise, what it is done in the fall with anticipation for what is planned for the following spring, and so it goes. The year-end harvest, however, was the high point of the year. It determined whether your labor over the past several months proved to be profitable or futile. Regardless, the harvest signaled a time for rest until a break in the winter weather came so that the cycle could begin again.

In the Parable of the Seed, Jesus demonstrates that the Reign of God has this cyclical or progressive quality. It suggests that growth resulting from the Reign of God begins gradually, continues in an orderly manner, is mysterious, and brings about finality.

Jesus said, "This is what the Kingdom of God is like. A man scatters seed on the ground. Night and day, whether he sleeps or gets up, the seed sprouts and grows, though he does not know how. All by itself, the soil produces grain—first the stalk, then the head, and then the full kernel in the head. He puts the sicks soon as the grain is ripe because the harvest has come."

Application

The audience has not changed. It follows Jesus' interpretation of the Parable of the Sower and his discussion of the key to understanding the parables. When using the same metaphor, the rabbis connected the seed with the study of the Torah. Its closeness to the Parable of the Sower suggests the seed is likewise the message of the Reign of God. The man scattering the seed is not identified. Some say this farmer represents the Son of Man, as in the Parable of the Weeds in the Field (Matt. 13:37). But his identity seems to be a secondary detail. Perhaps he represents anyone who possesses the message of the Kingdom. This parable seems to explain the dynamics of the previous parable and the abundant harvest from the good soil. This parable introduces us to the internal power and activity of the Reign of God.

The completed picture insists upon the involvement of three elements—the man who sows, the seed, and the soil. Yet, Jesus may be emphasizing a fourth element implied in the phrase *all by itself*. The phrase *by itself* is from the Greek word *automatos*. The only other time this word is used in the Greek New Testament is in Acts 12:10, which tells of when Peter was miraculously freed from prison. The passage states that the iron gates that led to the city opened *by themselves* (*automatos*). This word is also found in Joshua 6:5 of the Septuagint (LXX, the Greek translation of the Hebrew Bible). Speaking of the walls of Jericho, God tells Joshua, "When they [the Israelites] have shouted, the walls of the city shall fall of themselves." The apparent insinuation, of course, is God's direct operation. If these passages share this same intent, then the parable possesses an unseen element—the presence and activity of God.

In Jewish thought, it went without saying that God controls the sowing, the germination, the growth, and the abundance of the harvest. For that reason, prayers were on the lips of the Jews during every stage of sowing and harvesting. They believed that nothing could be expected without God's personal activity. The apostle Paul and his fellow worker, Apollos, express this sentiment. They considered themselves as merely co-workers with God while trusting him to give them an increase from their labors. "Neither he who plants nor he who waters is anything," Paul said (1 Cor. 3:6–7). The prevailing thought was that God is the One in control. Therefore, the Kingdom of God and everything resulting from it was believed to depend solely upon him. The most righteous Jew could not, by his faith and good deeds, override God's timing or process nor work out an appeasement to gain his favor—keep in mind that there were those who thought otherwise. He understood that it was all by

God's good grace. Ultimately, growth and the that which is produced are completely out of human hands.

What Harvest?

First, rabbinic teaching often equated judgment with the concept of harvest, especially in Jewish apocalyptic literature of the late Second Temple period because it was a biblical metaphor for judgment used by the Old Testament prophets. One such passage this parable brings to mind is Joel 3:9–13.

> Proclaim this among the nations: Prepare for war! Rouse the warriors! Let all the fighting men draw near and attack. Beat your plowshares into swords and your pruning hooks into spears. Let the weakling say, 'I am strong!' Come quickly, all you nations from every side, and assemble there. Bring down your warriors, O LORD! Let the nations be roused; let them advance into the Valley of Jehoshaphat, for there I will sit to judge all the nations on every side. Swing the sickle, for the harvest is ripe.

This passage deals with God's judgment upon the nations described as the "day of the LORD," saying the "harvest is ripe." John the Baptizer spoke of the Messiah as the Judge with a winnowing fork (Matt. 3:12; Luke 3:17.). James also uses the judgment-harvest theme. As an encouragement for persecuted Christians, he urges them to be patient and to await the coming of the Lord of Sabaoth, who is ready at the door to judge their oppressors (James 5:7–8). The nearness of judgment in each of these passages is an interesting detail that goes along with the preparation for harvest. Therefore, the harvest was viewed as a judgment in first-century Jewish teaching.

Second, Jesus speaks of preaching as harvesting (Matt. 9:37–38; Luke 10:2; John 4:35, 38.). Jeremias makes this point by saying, "The interpretation of 'sowing' as preaching is not characteristic of Jesus' way of speaking; he prefers to compare preaching with the gathering in of the harvest" (78). Therefore, while we sometimes sing the song that asks, "Are you sowing the seed of the Kingdom in the morning bright and fair," preaching is more of a form of harvesting. It certainly has a way of separating and gathering. Any preacher of the gospel will testify of having experienced this many times. I recall the story of a man baptized into Christ after hearing the gospel. The preacher went home with him to share the good news with the man's wife. But when she heard the news, she told the preacher that, as far as she was concerned, he might as well have brought her husband home in a pine box. Yes, preaching the gospel of Christ does produce very different responses that correspond with the harvest theme of gathering or separating.

Third, righteousness is sometimes viewed in Scripture as a kind of harvest. The righteousness of God is not mentioned in these parables but must be implied with any reference to the Kingdom of God. Where God's reign is, his righteousness dwells. Therefore, we may contend that the harvest in view here is God's righteousness rather than judgment or preaching. God expects a harvest of righteousness from his people. In Paul's prayer for the Corinthian church, God is viewed as able to supply them with the seed and increase the fruits of their righteousness (2 Cor. 8:10.). He also prayed that God might fill the church in Philippi with fruits of righteousness (Phil. 1:11). The Book of Hebrews speaks of God's discipline as a means of producing the "peaceable fruit of righteousness" (12:11). These all speak of a harvest theme with righteousness in view.

But faith is not to be confused with the Reign of God. Faith is the result of his reign, which allows his reign to remain unchanging while our faith grows in stages. Whether a kingdom person has been in Christ for one day or for 70 years, the Reign of God resides in both. Our faith will demonstrate a marked difference in growth and maturity.

So, what is the harvest in this parable? Any of the four considerations mentioned are good choices and have scriptural backing. However, the combination of faith and righteousness is more applicable. The message in this series of parables seems to be progressing toward an indictment and condemnation of those who are defiant, faithless, and void of righteousness. Assuming this is the direction that Jesus is going, the lack of faith and righteousness will be the cause for judgment upon the Jewish establishment.

Transformation:
The Mystery of the Reign of God

How the germ of life is reproduced within a seed is a marvel of nature, if not still somewhat of a mystery. Grains of wheat have been found in the tombs of Egypt that, when planted, sprouted. Anyone who sows a seed knows that it is not the ability of the one doing the sowing that causes the seed to germinate. He only facilitates the process. He simply trusts that the right elements will come together in just the right combination, producing the desired result. The seed will sprout according to God's natural design, regardless of whether we have faith.

Jesus says it is the same with the Reign of God. Our faith and knowledge are non-essentials when speaking of specific dimensions of the Kingdom of God and are not prerequisites for his activity. Again, faith is the thing produced. So then, the Reign of God may work independently of our human understanding or involvement. Yet, when we choose to become involved, the Reign of God has the ability to transform. This transformation is the result of the internal workings of the Kingdom as our submission to the Reign of God becomes like a seed exposed to soil, water, and sunlight. Only then can God expect to harvest faith and righteousness to his glory.

Food for Thought

1. What quality seems to be highlighted in the Parable of the Seed?

2. Discuss using the word *automatos* in Mark's narrative and how it agrees with the Jewish belief in God's involvement.

3. Discuss the four possibilities for the harvest and what it appears to be from the context.

4. Discuss this statement. "Our faith and knowledge are non-essentials when speaking of certain dimensions of the Kingdom of God and are not prerequisites for his activity."

5. If the Reign of God is not produced, what is?

6. What occurs when we become involved with the Reign of God?

7. What is the most meaningful thing you learned from this lesson?

Chapter 9

The Parable of the Weeds in the Field

Matthew 13:24–30; 36–43

Nothing is more frustrating for a farmer than to deal with the reoccurrence of weeds thought to have been eradicated. I remember my father's aggravation with a neighboring farmer who allowed his thistles to bloom in the field, joining ours. Thistles are relentless. When they go to seed, their tiny seeds take to the wind, carried by little white cotton-like parachutes. You can depend on a fresh crop the following summer. This parable does not deal with thistles, but it does deal with an unwanted noxious weed. What is worse, these seeds were maliciously sown. Here is the parable with its interpretation:

Jesus told them another parable:

> The Kingdom of heaven is like a man who sowed good seed in his field. But while everyone was sleeping, his enemy came and sowed weeds among the wheat and went away. When the wheat sprouted and formed heads, then the weeds also appeared. The owner's servants came to him and said, "Sir, didn't you sow good seed in your field? Where then did the weeds come from?" "An enemy did this," he replied. The servants asked him, "Do you want us to go and pull them up?" "No," he answered, "because while you are pulling the weeds, you may root up the wheat with them. Let both grow together until the harvest. At that time I will tell the harvesters: First collect the weeds and tie them in bundles to be burned; then gather the wheat and bring it into my barn.

Jesus gave the interpretation of this parable, which is recorded in Matthew 13:36–43.

> The one who sowed the good seed is the Son of Man. The field is the world, and the good seed stands for the sons of the Kingdom. The weeds are the sons of the evil one, and the enemy who sows them is the devil. The harvest is the end of the age, and the harvesters are angels. As the weeds are pulled up and burned in the fire, so it will be at the end of the age. The Son of Man will send out his angels, and they will weed out of his kingdom everything that causes sin and all who do evil. They will throw them into the fiery furnace, where there will be weeping and gnashing of teeth. Then the righteous will shine like the sun in the Kingdom of their Father. He who has ears, let him hear.

Middle Eastern Background

This parable has the same Middle Eastern harvest theme that was frequently used in the Jewish teaching of Jesus' day. Harvest was a time to separate wheat or barley from the weeds and chaff. The sheaves were gathered and taken to the threshing floor, leaving the weeds in the field to be gathered and burned or else saved as fuel. The weed of this parable is thought to be *darnel*. (There is an interesting play on the Hebrew word *zunin*.[10] Refer to the note on this). Darnel is a member of the Ryegrass family. It resembles wheat until it matures. It grows exclusively in grain fields throughout the Middle East (Wenham 57). It has a strong root system that grows stronger and deeper than that of wheat. So, it is true that removing it would uproot any wheat growing next to it. According to ancient Judaism, because of the resemblance darnel has with wheat, it was not considered a different variety of plant. Darnel was thought to be "a kind of wheat, which changed in the earth, both as to its form and its nature" (Lightfoot II:215). Of course, it is not a different variety of wheat. It is a noxious weed infected by a poisonous fungus, making its seed harmful if ingested.

Details, Phrases, and Their Significance

This parable is packed with Hebrew themes, idioms, and familiar Jewish images. Let's disassemble the parables and examine them individually. Each detail and phrase has significance. Bear with me because it is necessary to explore nuances that were known when Jesus spoke this parable. This is not to say that everyone in his audience would have been educated well enough to know each detail's significance. Most of them did not, but the scribes and experts in the Law would have been exposed to these things. Furthermore, the prophets were read alongside the Torah each Sabbath. One would think that the details and phrases of this parable would have been introduced at this point.

Jewish Phrases and their Significance: Son of Man

The first one is the title *Son of Man*. No other phrase expressed the humanity of the Messiah more than this one. In Jewish thought, the *Son of Man* was connected with the Suffering Servant of Isaiah, chapters 40–55. The Suffering Servant and the *Son of Man* possess the same human element that joins the Coming One with his people and their human experience. The context of Isaiah chapters 40–55 speaks of Israel as God's suffering servant. However, by the time of Jesus, the Jews had personified these references to Israel collectively into one individual—the Messiah. Jesus acknowledges their use of this passage by applying it to himself. After his resurrection, he appeared to the disciples, asking, "Did not the Christ have to suffer these things and then enter his glory?" He went on to say to them, "This is what is written: The Christ will suffer and rise from the dead on the third day" (Luke 24:26, 46). As the Son of Man, Jesus identified himself with the Suffering Servant of Isaiah. Later, the apostle Peter wrote concerning our salvation in Jesus, saying that the prophets spoke by the Spirit of the Messiah who was in them when he [Messiah] predicted his sufferings and the glories that followed (1 Peter 1:12).

In Jewish apocalyptic literature of the late Second Temple period, the title *Son of Man* also carried supernatural, divine, and immortal characteristics. The *Son of Man* was envisioned with more-than-human attributes. I am not trying to put Jewish literature on the same level as scripture. However, a brief reference to one source may help us understand what they expected from the *Son of Man*. An example is from the First Book of Enoch, a well-read and widely-known apocalyptic work of that period. The *Son of Man* is described as being with God and to be revealed to the elect:

> And with him [God] was another being whose countenance had the appearance of a man, and his face was full of graciousness like one of the holy angels (1 Enoch 46:1–2).

> "From eternity was the Son of Man concealed, whom the Most High preserved in the presence of his power and revealed to the elect. [… All souls] "shall fix their hopes on this Son of Man. They shall pray to him and petition him for mercy." [These elect shall] "dwell, eat, lie down, and rise up forever with this Son of Man" (1 Enoch 61:9–18)

Jesus takes these implied God-like attributes a step further by declaring the Son of Man as Deity and making this title one of his strongest claims of Deity. For example, the *Son of Man* and *I AM* are tied closely together. *"So Jesus said, 'When you have lifted up the **Son of Man**, then you will know that **I am the one I claim to be**'"* (John 8:28, emphasis mine). By stating that he is I AM, he declared that the *Son of Man* was Yahweh, the God of Israel. The Messianic allusions in Daniel's prophecy and Luke's gospel both agreed that the *Son of Man* has attributes of Deity who would come with the clouds in judgment. Daniel writes:

> In my vision at night I looked, and there before me was one like a Son of Man, coming with the clouds of heaven. He approached the Ancient of Days and was led into his presence. He was given authority, glory and sovereign power; all peoples, nations and men of every language worshiped him. His dominion is an everlasting dominion that will not pass away, and his kingdom is one that will never be destroyed (Dan. 7:13–14).

Jesus attributed Daniel's vision of the *Son of Man* to himself. He declared, "At that time they will see the Son of Man coming in a cloud with power and great glory" (Luke 21:24). Jesus attributed the title *Son of Man* from Daniel 7:13 to himself.

Therefore, ancient Judaism recognized the title *Son of Man* as the Messianic title of the One who sits as Judge of the nations and as the Redeemer of Israel. This Messianic title in the Parable of the Weeds in the Field undoubtedly refers to Jesus.

Sons of the Kingdom and Sons of the Evil One

The *sons of the Kingdom* are an apparent reference to the righteous remnant of Israel. They are presented in contrast to the *sons of the evil one*. Who do they represent? There exists a parable called *The Argument of the Wheat and the Tares*[11] that may give us some indication. This parable emphasized the Jewish relationship with Gentiles.

The tares said to the wheat, "We are more beautiful than you are. The rain falls for us and for you, and the sun shines on both of us." The wheat said to the tares, "It is not important what you say, nor is it important what we say; but rather the winnowing fan because it comes and separates us for the storehouse, and you for the birds to eat."

This illustrates the attitude of the Jewish leadership. However, Jesus does not address the Jewish and Gentile relationship in his parable. It was not the Gentiles who were causing sin and doing evil in the way Jesus is implying. It was the Jewish leadership that was a stumbling block to those who were becoming believers in Jesus. In John 8:44, Jesus accused the Pharisees of being sons of the devil. Therefore, this indictment seems to be directed against the Jewish Sanhedrin. They are the sons of the evil one. Jesus is giving the same stern warning that will be given later against those who cause his disciples to stumble, saying, "It would be better for him to have a millstone hung around his neck and to be drowned in the depths of the sea."

Angels

Belief in *angels* was common in Jewish tradition, though not all believed in their existence. Some ancient Jewish sects of the first century speak of them as administrators of God's will and executioners of God's judgment, such as apocalyptic literature like the first Book of Enoch, which speaks of angels as active agents of God's judgment. A thorough study of the Old Testament prophets on the activity of angels should help prevent our Western tendency from automatically interpreting this parable as an end-of-time prophecy.

Certainly, the angels of God *will* be active at the end of time when Christ returns, but they have been active in the execution of judgment upon nations of the earth since the dawn of human history. Angelic activity is mentioned in the language of judgment upon pagan nations throughout the Bible. For example, angelic activity is seen in the visions of Ezekiel concerning God's judgment among the nations and the first destruction of Jerusalem by the Babylonians in 586 B.C. Angelic activity is seen in Daniel's visions regarding the rise and fall of the Babylonians, the Medo-Persians, and the Greeks. Angelic activity is also seen in John's visions in the Book of Revelation, which predict the judgment and fall of the beast—the Roman Empire. Angels are pictured as reapers with sickles, bringing in the harvest or pouring out bowls of wrath. Unlike the Western view of angels as being harmless, feminine, and childlike, the very mention of angelic activity would have communicated to the first-century Jewish imagination visions of God's execution of judgment on the earth. They were feared.

We must also remember that angelic references in apocalyptic literature are highly figurative. The listener or reader is expected to understand the message by viewing the overall picture without getting lost in the details. The key to interpreting apocalyptic language is remembering that the message is *painting a picture through symbols*.

Executing judgment is not the only function of angels. In both the Old and New Testaments, angels are said to worship in God's presence (Isa. 6:2–3; Rev. 4:8; 5:11–12). They also advocate for the "little ones" of the Messiah in some way before the throne (Matt. 18:10). They are also spoken of as "ministering spirits sent to serve those who will inherit salvation" (Heb. 1:14) Angels share at least two characteristics with human beings. (1) Adam was created as a spiritual being. (2) Angels and humans are subject to the Law of Sin and Death (Ezek. 18:4b). The difference is that human beings can be delivered from the Law of Sin and Death; angels cannot. According to the first book of Enoch, the Letter of Jude, and the second letter of the apostle Peter, angels who have sinned are eternally banished from God's presence without hope of being redeemed (1 Enoch 6–10; Jude 6; 2 Pet. 2:4).

There are other uses of the word *angel* in Hebrew. For instance, the term *angel* can refer to a *man of God* or a *messenger of God*. The Greek word *angelos* and its corresponding Hebrew word can be translated as messenger and, at times, refers to men of God rather than heavenly beings. For example, Matthew 11:10 uses it to speak of John the Baptizer. Luke 7:24 is used to speak of the disciples of John the Baptizer. In Luke 9:52, Jesus' disciples are called messengers (*angelos*). In James 2:25, the same word is used for the two spies at Rahab's house. In early Judaism, the synagogue's leader was called the Angel of the assembly (Lightfoot II:90–1). Interestingly, the pulpit minister was called *angelos*, the *angel*. Compare this with Jesus' address to the seven churches of Asia in the Book of Revelation.

Therefore, angels may be heavenly or human, depending on the context. Their activity may suggest their literal involvement or may be a part of a picture symbolizing God's judgment. Whether it is literal or intended to be figurative language, the main point of this parable is clear. Jesus reveals that, as the Son of Man, he is the Commander of these special messengers. More will be added to this subject in a moment.

End of the Age

Another familiar phrase Jesus uses in this parable is the *end of the age*. It is used only five times and exclusively by Matthew (13:39– 40, 49; 24:3; 28:20.). The word *age* is from the Greek word *aionos* and refers to a dispensation in time. The *end of the age* contained Messianic overtones in Jewish eschatology. Eschatology is the study of the *end of days*. Generally speaking, first-century Jewish eschatology and early Christian eschatology focused on different things, but both essentially had two things in common. Both belief systems view time as linear and look for new heavens and new earth with the advent of the Messiah. The Jews looked for the heralding of the Messiah's arrival with the new age. As Christians, we believe Jesus of Nazareth is God incarnate who was crucified, buried, raised, and enthroned as the Messiah. We are now awaiting his second coming, the bodily resurrection, the world's destruction, the judgment of all men, and the reward of the righteous of the ages in heaven. Variations in the details of these events are taught across the eschatological landscape with far-reaching implications. Still, the end of the present world and a new beginning are taught universally.

The ancient Jewish teaching of the end of days did not necessarily involve the destruction of the earth. It involved God's enemies being destroyed, the appearance of Elijah and the Messiah, the gathering of Israel back to Jerusalem where it is believed the Temple will be rebuilt, the resurrection of the dead, and judgment. According to ancient Jewish tradition, it will be an age of holiness, justice, and spiritual renewal where the Messiah is inaugurated as King of Israel. A new creation was expected, but not a catastrophic cosmic event.

The rabbis of the late Second Temple period interpreted such passages as Jeremiah 10:25 with an end-of-the-age worldview. They interpreted many scriptures that spoke of judgment with an *end-of-days* application. In other words, they figured that what God did for his people in the past would be repeated in the future. Jeremiah 10:25 reads:

Pour out your wrath on the nations that do not acknowledge you, on the peoples who do not call on your name. For they have devoured Jacob; they have devoured him completely and destroyed his homeland.

Jeremiah was asking for judgment upon Babylon. However, the rabbis of the late Second Temple period viewed this passage as speaking equally of Rome. As Babylon had devoured Jacob in Jeremiah's day, Rome had devoured Jacob and destroyed his homeland in Jesus' day. Therefore, Rome deserved God's wrath as much as the Babylonians did. The rabbis believed this judgment would occur at the *end of days*, or in the *age to come*, and correspond with the days of Messiah and the restoration of the Kingdom to Israel. Therefore, the phrase *end of the age* refers to the end of a dispensation of time.

Food for Thought

1. Discuss the custom of harvesting in ancient times. Think about how wheat was separated from the weeds.

2. What kind of weed is most likely described in this parable?

3. Discuss the Jewish implication brought to mind with the phrase *Son of Man*.

4. How does Jesus raise the level of identity as the Son of Man to Deity?

5. The rabbis, through a parable similar to the Parable of the Weeds and the Wheat, implied that the Gentiles are the sons of the evil one. Discuss your opinion on who the sons of the evil one are in this parable.

6. What is the definition of the word *eschatology*?

7. What two things do Jewish and Christian eschatology have in common?

8. What particular mission of angels is revealed from the Old Testament?

9. What does the Greek word *angelos* mean? How else is the word *angelos* used in the Bible? Give references for your answer.

10. The phrase *end of the age* has been interpreted as the end of the world and even translated as such in a couple of versions of the Bible. Discuss why this is incorrect.

11. What is the most meaningful thing you learned from this lesson?

Chapter 10

Kingdom of Heaven and Kingdom of Their Father

The terms *the Kingdom of Heaven* and *the Kingdom of their Father* are very Jewish. The Jews used euphemisms when speaking of God and in place of his holy name. It is forbidden by Jewish law to utter the covenant name of God. This is why Jesus used the phrase *Kingdom of Heaven*. The word *heaven* was in direct reference to God. The phrase *Kingdom of God* is not found in Jewish literature of that period. Only the phrase *Kingdom of Heaven* is found. Matthew uses this euphemism more than Mark or Luke. As for the reason why Mark and Luke use the alternate phrase *Kingdom of God*, it is believed that their Greek readers would not have understood the Hebrew euphemism.

The term *Kingdom of their Father* is likewise a common euphemism for God. It was common in Jewish prayers in the synagogue to address God as **our** Father. According to their tradition, however, it was forbidden to address God as **my** Father, as Jesus did numerous times, creating quite a stir because the Jews regarded this as making oneself equal to God (see John 5:18.). Jesus taught his disciples to pray in a standard Jewish tradition when he instructed them to address God as "Our Father" (Matt. 6:9; Luke 11:2.) Using the possessive determiner was characteristic of Jewish prayer. There is nothing new or unusual here. Therefore, the phrase *kingdom of their Father* was a common euphemism referring to God and his reign.

Weeping and Gnashing of Teeth

The expression *weeping and gnashing of teeth* is used seven times in the Gospels. These words are more often thought to imply unending conscious suffering in Gehenna. But it might be surprising to learn that this idiomatic expression is used in various contexts, ranging from extreme sorrow and distress to hatred expressed by an adversary.

- Isaiah 22:12 speaks of when Babylon would destroy Jerusalem, where God calls for mournful repentance.
- The Book of Lamentations contains expressions similar to those of Jeremiah, who lamented the destruction of Jerusalem by Babylon.
- In Psalm 112:10, the Psalmist uses the exact figure of speech to describe the anger of the wicked against the good deeds of the righteous.
- Job viewed God as angry with him and gnashing his teeth at him (Job 16:9).
- It describes an enemy's hot anger (Psalm 35:16; 37:12; Lamentations 2:16, and Acts 7:54).
- James 5:1 uses the same language, telling the rich who oppress the poor to weep and mourn for fear of God's imminent judgment upon them.
- Revelation 18:9 speaks of pagan kings lamenting the destruction of Rome.
- In Matthew 24:51, Jesus used this figure of speech to describe the extreme torment and suffering that would come with the A.D. 70 destruction of Jerusalem.

This could refer to unending torment in hell, but the context must always determine our interpretation. Therefore, because of the various applications of this expression in scripture, it would be unwise to read into this parable an *end-time* application without first considering the extent of its use within its context.

Immediate Application of the Wheat and the Weeds

The Parable of the Weeds in the Field is universally interpreted as speaking of the world's end and the Second Coming of Christ. That may be applicable as a principle since the language of judgment is essentially the same. But we have to consider another application. It seems more logically placed within a series of warnings by Jesus about the approaching destruction of Jerusalem. There are over 120 passages of scripture in the Old and New Testaments, specifically prophesying and describing the event of the A.D. 70 destruction of Jerusalem as occurring in the last days. This was such a major event that Jesus spent much of his ministry warning of its imminent approach and calling for Israel's repentance. The A.D. 70 destruction was the end of the Jewish era. The descriptive language Jesus used in this parable is very similar to that used in his discourse on the destruction of Jerusalem from Matthew 24, Mark 13, Luke 17, and Luke 21. He predicts and describes his judgment upon Jerusalem, using ancient Jewish apocalyptic language of judgment. The following point should help to make this even more self-evident.

First, Pull the Weeds

There is a peculiar detail in this parable that is worth noting. Matthew 13:30 of the Parable of the Weeds in the Field reads, "At that time I will tell the harvesters: First collect the weeds and tie them in bundles to be burned." It is the order of the harvest that is unusual if this is talking about the end of the world. The wicked are taken away *first,* leaving the righteous to be gathered later. Comparing this to Jesus' discourse on the Matthew 24 event, we find a similar order. Jesus said, Matt. 24:37, *"As in the days of Noah,* so it will be at the coming of the Son of Man" (emphasis mine). The Flood took away the wicked, and the righteous (Noah and his family) were left. Jesus said the event of Matthew 24 is expected to parallel the Flood event in that the wicked will be taken away, leaving the righteous. If this parable is intended to be understood as a prediction of the order of things at the Second Coming, this does not agree with Paul's description. According to Paul, the final coming of Christ is a single event when *all* the righteous will be taken first and the wicked left. Paul says (1 Thess. 4:16–17)—

> According to the Lord's own word, we tell you that we who are still alive, who are left till the coming of the Lord, will certainly not precede those who have fallen asleep. For the Lord himself will come down from heaven, with a loud command, with the voice of the archangel and with the trumpet call of God, and **the dead in Christ will rise first**. After that, we who are still alive and are left will be caught up together with them in the clouds to

meet the Lord in the air. And so we will be with the Lord forever (emphasis mine).

So, why is the order in the parable and Matthew 24 different? The reason is that Matthew 24 and the Parable of the Weeds in the Field describe the same historical event—the A.D. 70 collapse of the Jewish nation. I can't see it predicting the Second Coming of Christ as the immediate application. Between A.D. 66–68, Jewish Christians fled about 60 miles northeast of Jerusalem to Pella, located in Perea (Wilson 76), leaving behind hundreds of thousands of unbelieving Jews who died in the inferno of the city's destruction. The Parable of the Weeds in the Field says that the sons of the evil one are taken and destroyed, while the sons of the Kingdom are left for gathering.

The gathering of God's people is a common expression of Divine deliverance from persecution and captivity. Deuteronomy 30:3 is the promise from God that he will gather his people from all the nations where he has scattered them. It was a prophecy of the restoration of the nation. Isaiah 43:5 offers reassurance from God, who promises to gather his people from the East and the West. Then there is Jeremiah 32:37 and Ezekiel 34:11–13, both of which speak of another promise from God. He will gather his people from exile among the nations to return them to Jerusalem. When God called or gathered his people, he did so by messengers like the prophets and other spiritual leaders. It is plausible that the angels in this parable are men of God whom he used to gather his people, leading them from the destruction of Jerusalem to safety across the Jordan River before A. D. 70. Again, angels in the Bible do not always refer to heavenly beings. Therefore, pulling the weeds (removing the sons of the evil one) and leaving the righteous to be gathered later indicate a national judgment in history rather than a universal judgment at the end of time.

The End of the Age—When?

Earlier, I mentioned that the *end of the age* signaled the end of one era and the beginning of another. Some versions of the Bible translate the word *aionos* as the end of the *world*. This is unfortunate because it has contributed to a misinterpretation of several passages. The end of the age may not speak of the *end of the world*. The context has to be considered.

Too often, the context is made to fit the presumption. The starting point when interpreting the end of the age is that it refers to *the end of the life of a nation*. In Matthew's narrative, it is the end of the Jewish nation and the termination of the Jewish government. Two other Greek words are translated as *"world* in the Gospel of Matthew. The word *kosmos* is used in Matthew 13:35 to refer to the *orderly arrangement of the universe.* The word *oikoumene* in Matthew 24:14 relates to the *people of the world.* But it is *aionos* that refers to *an era of time.* My friend, Sammy Flanary (46–7), explained the meaning of the *end of the age* like this:

> Contextually, it is the ending of the Jewish age. In promise, it began with Abraham. In development, it became a reality through Jacob or *Israel.* God, through his servant, Daniel, promised that the nation and the city of Jerusalem would come to a full end (Daniel 9:27). It would be the ending of the Jewish eras of time for the nation ...

Therefore, as Jesus intended in this parable, the end of the age speaks of a historical event when the end of the Jewish age occurred. Many will disagree with me, but everything points in one direction. It can only be the destruction of Jerusalem in A.D. 70.

The Sons of the Kingdom Will Be Vindicated

Jesus said that the *righteous will shine like the sun in the Kingdom at the end of the age.* In ancient Jewish thought, this spoke of vindication of the righteous. Compare this with Psalm 37:1–6.

> Do not fret because of evil men or be envious of those who do wrong; for like the grass they will soon wither, like green plants they will soon die away. Trust in the LORD and do good; dwell in the land and enjoy safe pasture. Delight yourself in the LORD and he will give you the desires of your heart. Commit your way to the LORD; trust in him and he will do this: He will make your righteousness shine like the dawn, the justice of your cause like the noonday sun.

This same exhortation was communicated to the Jewish exiles during the days of Ezekiel, who needed to hear that the truth of God would be vindicated. First-century Jewish believers in Jesus witnessed the destruction of the Temple and Jerusalem. They likewise needed to know their faith would be vindicated. They needed to hear words reminiscent of the prophets who said things like, *"the righteous will shine like the sun in the Kingdom."*

This echoes Malachi 4:1–6, which looks ahead to the time element of the A.D. 70 destruction of Jerusalem and predicts the coming of John the Baptizer:

> "Surely the day is coming; it will burn like a furnace. All the arrogant and every evildoer will be stubble, and that day that is coming will set them on fire," says the Lord Almighty. "Not a root or a branch will be left to them. But for you who revere my name, **the sun of righteousness will rise with healing in its wings.**[12] And you will go out and leap like calves released from the stall. Then you will trample down the wicked; they will be ashes under the soles of your feet on the day when I do these things," says the Lord Almighty. "Remember the law of my servant Moses, the decrees and laws I gave him at Horeb for all Israel. See, I will send you the prophet Elijah before that great and dreadful day of the Lord comes. He will turn the hearts of the fathers to their children, and the hearts of the children to their fathers; or else I will come and strike the land with a curse." (emphasis mine)

Malachi foretold that *"the **sun of righteousness** will rise with healing in its wings."* This passage is clearly Messianic, with a promise of vindication. The righteous ones of God throughout history will always need a constant reminder that says the righteousness they uphold and the truth upon which they stand will be vindicated.

We must not conclude without referring to Daniel 12:3. The phrase, *"the righteous will shine like the sun in the Kingdom,"* was also an obvious allusion to Daniel's words, who used this language to say that the *"wise will shine like the brightness of the heaven."* Daniel's prophecy looked ahead to the persecution of Israel by Antiochus Epiphanes IV. Three centuries before Antiochus defiled the Temple of Jerusalem, God gave hope to those who would remain faithful and that their faith would be vindicated in the resurrection.

The righteous in this context are those who remain faithful through the days of tribulation surrounding the collapse of the Jewish nation in A.D. 70. The Parable of the Weeds in the Field was a stern warning to the Jewish people. Those who failed to submit to God's reign through Jesus, the Messiah, suffered his judgment. As for his believers, their righteousness in the Reign of God would not be forgotten, nor would their suffering be in vain.

Summary

- The Parable of the Weeds in the Field seems to follow a logical sequence when it is combined with the previous two parables with an overall message that warns of judgment.
- The Parable of the Sower emphasizes the importance of hearing and practicing the message of the Reign of God.
- The Parable of the Seed illustrates the presence and activity of the Reign of God. It emphasizes the importance of the harvest of faith and righteousness produced from practicing the message of the Reign of God.
- Consequently, the Parable of the Weeds in the Field warns the Jewish elite of judgment for failing to hear the message of the Kingdom, practice it, and produce faith and righteousness as a nation. Failure to practice the Reign of God invokes judgment individually and nationally.

Application for Us

Although this parable is directed toward those of Jesus' day as a warning, we in Christ remain in a world filled with unbelievers. There will be a time of harvest and judgment for all humanity. But as long as we are in the world, it is the mission of the "wheat" to take the message of the Kingdom into the "weeds" of the world. It might not be possible for weeds in the botanical world to be transformed into wheat, but human beings can be transformed. Jesus said that the righteous are exempt from judgment (John 5:4). There is no condemnation as long as we remain faithful to Christ (Rom. 8:1, 29). One last thing: the truth of God embodied in the sons of the Kingdom will always be vindicated, and the righteous will always shine like the sun in the Reign of God.

Food for Thought

1. What was the common Jewish address to God in synagogue prayers and what was forbidden in Judaism?

2. How does the order of the harvest parallel the days of Noah mentioned in Matthew 24:37?

3. Discuss the plausible explanation of who the angels could represent in the parable.

4. Discuss the historical events that this parable seems to be predicting.

5. Discuss how this parable follows a logical progression of the previous parables.

6. What Messianic promise may be attached to the phrase *the righteous will shine like the sun in the Kingdom*? Discuss how this promise is valid for us today.

7. 10. What is the most meaningful thing you learned from this lesson?

Chapter 11

The Parables of the Mustard Seed and the Yeast

Matthew 13:31–33; Mark 4:31–32; Luke 13:19–21

The first three parables have emphasized the message of the Kingdom. The seed was sown in four types of soil, representing four kinds of hearers. We have seen how the Reign of God mysteriously germinates and that which grows out of the Reign of God develops in stages of maturity until it is ready for harvest. Finally, we heard a warning about judgment. A more contextualized interpretation of the Parable of the Weeds in the Field leads us to understand that the righteous faith of the Jewish believer in the Messiah will be vindicated. At the same time, unbelievers (the sons of the evil one) will be judged.

The following two parables in this discourse are typically called twin parables. They are combined to illustrate the greatness and worth of the Reign of God to kingdom people.

The Parable of the Mustard Seed

MATTHEW 13:31–32

He told them another parable: "The Kingdom of heaven is like a mustard seed, which a man took and planted in his field. Though it is the smallest of all your seeds, yet when it grows, it is the largest of garden plants and becomes a tree, so that the birds of the air come and perch in its branches."

MARK 4:31-32

Again he said, "What shall we say the Kingdom of God is like, or what parable shall we use to describe it? It is like a mustard seed, which is the smallest seed you plant in the ground. Yet when planted, it grows and becomes the largest of all garden plants, with such big branches that the birds of the air can perch in its shade."

LUKE 13:19
Then Jesus asked, "What is the Kingdom of God like? What shall I compare it to? It is like a mustard seed, which a man took and planted in his garden. It grew and became a tree, and the birds of the air perched in its branches."

The Parable of the Yeast

MATTHEW 13:33
He told them still another parable: "The Kingdom of heaven is like yeast that a woman took and mixed into a large amount of flour until it worked all through the dough."

LUKE 13:20–21
Again, he asked, "What shall I compare the Kingdom of God to?

It is like yeast that a woman took and mixed into a large amount of flour until it worked all through the dough."

Jewish Background of the Mustard Seed and the Yeast

Mustard Seed

The two probable varieties of mustard plants illustrated here are black and white mustard. Both grow annually in Palestine, beginning in the late spring. By comparison, these are not the smallest of seeds in that region. The size of the black mustard seed ranges from 1.0 to 3.0 millimeters, or one-eighth of an inch. Oesterley observes that "the seed of the cypress tree is smaller. But the detail is unimportant; besides, in the East, the mustard seed was, and is, proverbially used as the ordinary designation for anything very small and insignificant; moreover, according to the popular Jewish conception, it *was* regarded as the smallest of all seeds" (76). The keyword in Oesterley's comment is *proverbial*. However, Jesus' description of its growth does not appear to be proverbial but literal. The maximum growth of the black mustard seed ranges from three feet to as much as eight and ten feet in height, according to various sources. Naturally, the larger the plant grows, the more tree-like it becomes, making it desirable for birds to nest in its branches.

Yeast

Yeast is a microscopic organism or unicellular fungi. It is the fermenting agent that gives bread dough its ability to rise. But according to the Torah, it was almost always forbidden in bread as an offering to the Lord. Metaphorically, yeast represented corruption and sin (Matt. 16:6, 12; 1 Cor. 5:6–7; Gal. 5:9). It symbolized the corruption and idolatry of Egypt.

For this reason, yeast was to be removed from the homes of Israel before Passover, and it also included any food or beverage. Anything alcoholic was removed because it takes yeast to cause fruit juice to ferment. This leads to the thought that the drink used at the last Passover in which Jesus instituted the Lord's Supper was fresh grape juice.

In the Parable of the Yeast, however, Jesus speaks of yeast in a positive way, which was not that uncommon in Jewish teaching. The rabbis compared the positive qualities of peace and the benefits of studying the Torah to the permeating action of yeast. Rabbi Joshua ben Levi taught, "Great is peace—for as peace is to the earth so is yeast to the dough" (Young 79).The Jewish sage Chaya bar Abba compared the working of yeast to the power of God's word. He taught that even if God's commandments were forsaken, as long as Israel studied the Torah, its living and active power had the ability to bring them back to God. So, in Jewish thought, the metaphorical use of yeast was both positive and negative.

His Audience

There are two audiences to consider here. In Matthew's account, the audience is the same as the previous parables spoken to the crowd before Jesus left the lake shore and re-entered the house with his disciples (Matt. 13:36). In Luke's account, these parables were spoken in a synagogue on a Sabbath Day. The contexts are different, but they share three elements that set the stage for the purpose of the parables.

1. Jesus healed someone oppressed by Satan who also had a physical defect. (Matthew 12:22; Luke 13:10–13)
2. Religious leaders opposed; Jesus rebuked their hypocrisy. (Matthew 12:24–37; Luke 13:14–17)
3. Jesus presented Kingdom Parables to teach his audience and expose his antagonists. (Matthew 13:3–50; Luke 13:18–21)

In Luke's account, Jesus taught in one of the synagogues of Galilee on a Sabbath Day during his later Judean ministry. Among those in the assembly was a woman with a "spirit of infirmity" (New King James Version) that had kept her disabled for eighteen years. Without hesitation, Jesus healed her. This did not set well with the ruler of the synagogue, who reacted with antagonism because this was on the Sabbath Day. Jesus accused him of hypocrisy and pointed out his absurd inconsistency, humiliating him and his colleagues. This thrilled the people, but it infuriated the Pharisees even more. At this opportunity, Jesus presented his parables of the mustard seed and the yeast.

Application

The immediate application to his audiences in Luke and Matthew and the application to us will be virtually the same. To help make the point easier to see, we will consider the event in Luke 13:10-21. First, it is important to note that in these contexts (Matthew and Luke), several were "bound" by Satan. For example, the ruler of the synagogue was as spiritually bound by Satan as much as the woman was physically. We might say that the woman's physical condition was a *visual parallel* illustrating the ruler's spiritual condition. He and his group of antagonists were crippled by their legalism. Legalism only has the power to blind and enslave. It does not have the power to set free. As the ruler of the synagogue epitomizes, legalism not only blinds a person from seeing God and his activity in people's lives but will also stand in the way of it. It violates the two great commandments—loving God and loving your neighbor. The ruler of the synagogue would have kept the woman bound because of his loveless law-keeping for fear of violating some self-imposed rule. Legalists only see the narrow observance of regulations as acts of worship. This is what makes legalism so harmful and so evil. The religious elite of Jesus' day had distorted their view of God by creating their own self-enthroned image of him and thereby glorified their pursuit of flawless performance.

Second, the conceit that legalism fosters is nothing short of condescending hatred. Their careless disposition displayed contempt for the *Shema* even though it was read publicly in the synagogue liturgy each Sabbath day. Alongside the *Shema*, its twin commandment to love your neighbor as yourself was repeated as a central theme in Jewish teaching. One of Judaism's most beloved teachers, Jewish Rabbi Akiva, is famous for saying, "Love your neighbor as yourself. This is the major principle of the Torah." The *twin commandments* and the observance of the Sabbath were not to be reinterpreted by legalism's perversion of grace. Jesus said the Sabbath was made for people, not people for the Sabbath (Matt. 12:8; Mark 2:27–28; Luke 6:5).

God intended for his kingdom's people to use the Sabbath by being free to express the Reign of God in worshipful and caring ways. God intended for the Sabbath to be the day of all days of the week when expressions of love for God and love for one's neighbor could be practiced liberally.

Therefore, as acts of benevolence, adoration, and remembrance of all God had done for Israel extol the God of the Sabbath, the *twin commandments* are honored and obeyed. By releasing this daughter of Abraham from her bondage, Jesus demonstrated that benevolence was an act of loving worship to God as much as offering sacrifices, prayers, and remembering the Sabbath to keep it holy. Jesus defied legalism's hatred by extending grace. God's teaching of grace from the *twin commandments* and the observance of the Sabbath never said, "Come and be healed on another day, not today."

With this as the backdrop, Jesus asked, "What is the Kingdom (Reign) of God like?" The depiction of an insignificant mustard seed that matures into a tree-sized plant and the image of the fermentation of bread dough are cast alongside a dramatic demonstration of the Reign of God, illustrating its refusal to be restrained or intimidated. When demonstrated through the *Shema* and its *twin commandment, God's reign* begins inward, extends outward, reaches upward, and spreads throughout, aggressively challenging the religious *status quo*. Here, we see the Reign of God compelled by the love mandate to loosen those bound and set captives free. The result is joy expressed in the glory of God. Therefore, we have illustrated in parabolic ways an emphasis upon the *Shema* as it relates to loving God and how that is expressed by serving others—confirming that observing the *Shema* in the believer's life is how the Reign of God is realized and shown.

Food for Thought

1. These twin parables are repeated on two occasions. What three things are in common with the two events that make these parables applicable?

2. Discuss how the woman's condition paralleled the spiritual condition of the synagogue ruler and the other antagonists.

3. How does legalism keep people "bound?"

4. Discuss how the *Shema* and its twin commandment were violated.

5. How was the spirit of the Sabbath, the *Shema,* and loving your neighbor as yourself intended to go together?

6. Discuss demonstrations of the Reign of God as acts of worship, both then and now.

7. What is the most meaningful thing you learned from this lesson?

Chapter 12

The Parables of the Hidden Treasure and the Pearl of Great Price

Matthew 13:44-46

The Parable of the Hidden Treasure and the Parable of the Pearl of Great Price is the second set of twin parables in our context. Once again, the context of these parables begins in Matthew 12:22 and Mark 3:20, where we read of Jesus healing the man who was demon-possessed, blind, and mute. The scene that unfolded, as described by the three evangelists, provided the background for the series of parables we are highlighting.

In the Parables of the Hidden Treasure and the Pearl of Great Price, we learn the immense value of God's reign in our lives. Upon finding the treasure, the discoverer is overjoyed and more than willing to surrender everything to possess it. Matthew is the only gospel writer to record these parables. Here are the parables that will serve as our text.

The Parable of the Hidden Treasure

The Kingdom of heaven is like treasure hidden in a field. When a man found it, he hid it again, and then in his joy went and sold all he had and bought that field (Matt. 13:44)

The Parable of the Pearl of Great Price

Again, the Kingdom of heaven is like a merchant looking for fine pearls. When he found one of great value, he went away and sold everything he had and bought it (Matt. 13:45–46).

The Jewish Background of the Hidden Treasure

Just as in the Parable of the Sower, to the Jewish ear of the first century, these two parables echoed the priority of the study of the Torah. This goes back to Solomon, who urged his son to search for an understanding of God's wisdom as one would search for hidden treasure (Prov. 2:1–6). This sense of value for the Torah resonates throughout ancient Jewish teachings, which is reflected here. Its worth was considered more precious than all of one's possessions. An example is a discussion between two rabbis as they traveled through Galilee. As the two passed by a plot of ground and an olive grove, Rabbi Jochanan mentioned how he once owned it but had sold his fields in order to devote his time to studying the Torah. Rabbi Chija became very upset because Rabbi Jochanan had nothing left to sustain him in his old age. "He answered, 'Chija, my son, is it a small thing in thine eyes that I sold everything that was created in six days [see Exodus 31:17], and in place thereof gained that which was given in forty days and forty nights?'" (Oesterley 82–3) This illustrates the supreme value the Jews placed on the study of the Torah. The rabbis believed that within the Torah was the Kingdom of God. By studying the Torah and the recital of the *Shema*, they thought they were brought into the Reign of God.

    We can assume that Jesus had this integral part of the Jewish faith in mind when speaking these parables. To excel in the study of the Torah was commendable and profitable. However, as important as it was to study the Torah, Jesus seems to have taken it a step further. Studying without the assimilation of the Reign of God in one's life is merely an academic exercise. It is a misplacement of values when we value the study of God's word more than demonstrating the Reign of God in one's life. These must go hand-in-hand.

There is another point that Jesus seems to make in these parables that deviates from rabbinic thought on the Kingdom. Oesterley makes the point that while sacrificing everything to possess something else was not uncommon, the idea of the Kingdom of God as a personal possession was a new concept. The kingdom was never spoken of as a possession. Instead, the Kingdom of God was thought of only as something to which one belonged or into which one entered (Oesterley 83). Once again, Jesus takes familiar Jewish images while redirecting their focus to envision new ways of thinking about the Kingdom of God.

The Ethical Question

During times of unrest, valuables were buried for protection against looters. Josephus, a first-century Jewish historian, wrote, "Gold and the silver and the rest of that most precious furniture which the Jews had … the owners treasured up underground against the uncertain fortunes of war" (Book 7, 5:2). The ancient Jews trusted the earth and caves as the safest storehouses for their valuables. It was not uncommon then to be plowing or digging in a field and stumble upon something of value (Barclay II:93–4). The ethical question of whether the man who discovered the treasure had a moral obligation to disclose his find is not a consideration in the parable. Jesus' audience would not have worried about the external details of the parable. They would have centered their attention on the purpose of the parable.

The Jewish Background of the Pearl of Great Price

Pearls in the ancient world were not only natural wonders but were valued more than any other gem. The most precious pearls were fished out of the salty seas of the Middle and Far East, often at great risk to the diver's life. Only the very affluent owned pearls, making merchants very wealthy. A common villager might have only heard about their beauty and value since few could afford such exotic jewels in the first century. Still, the image of pearls in Jewish thought as a metaphor for something of great value and beauty was common, especially during the Hellenistic period. The rabbis used the pearl as a metaphor for beautifully spoken words. Jesus used the pearl metaphor, contrasting what is holy with what is unholy (Matt. 7:6). Pearls provided the perfect image for something of beauty and inestimable value.

Application

These two parables were spoken in the disciples' presence after leaving the crowd and re-entering the house. Again, these parables follow Jesus' interpretation of the Parable of the Weeds in the Field. Once again, as with the previous parables, the context begins with the events of Matthew 12:22, where, later in verse 28, Jesus announces, *"the Kingdom of God has come upon you."* In other words, the Reign of God was demonstrated with the power to transform and change lives. This leads us to something more about the effect of the Reign of God that needs to be added.

First, the quality of life is changed drastically because of the discovery and possession of the Reign of God. The two men in this parable immediately took inventory of their lives and concluded that their discoveries exceeded the value of everything they owned. They instantly envisioned the circumstances of their lives changing favorably. Suddenly, no price is too great to pay.

Second, because of the worth of the treasure and the priceless pearl, the question of sacrifice becomes negligible. The thought of sacrifice has taken on a negative connotation in our Western worldview. We often perceive sacrifice as giving up something of greater value for something of lesser value. In contrast, these parables teach us that what is gained from God's reign far outweighs and has far surpassing value over what we surrendered. Paul made a radical change when he gained Christ. He wrote, "I consider everything a loss compared to the surpassing greatness of knowing Christ Jesus my Lord, for whose sake I have lost all things. I consider them rubbish, that I may gain Christ and be found in him" (Phil. 3:8–9). Paul refused to place a price tag on what he had given up. This is the kind of radical change that Jesus wants of his disciples. The hidden spiritual treasure and the priceless spiritual pearl, representing God's reign within us through Jesus, bring a richness, happiness, and contentment that worldly wealth and false security cannot provide. Embracing the Reign of God is a wise investment.

The Hidden Treasure, the Pearl of Great Price, and the Shema

The *Shema* was such a central part of Jesus' teachings that we would be remiss to ignore it here. The Parables of the Hidden Treasure and the Pearl of Great Price speak of refocusing values. The refocusing of values was something Israel was expected to do every day, especially on the Sabbath day. The reading of the *Shema* was intended to direct the worshipper's attention to the Object of their affection—the God of Israel. This love-recital for God called the whole person into a single joyful investment toward God and to one another. His presence becomes the treasure and the coveted pearl for the worshipper who willingly surrenders all he has to gain it.

The twin commandment of the *Shema* involves loving your neighbor as yourself. Removing this element from a life transformed by gaining the hidden treasure and the priceless pearl is tantamount to trying to follow Jesus while refusing to serve others. The Reign of God in the kingdom person's life compels loving submission in service to others. Jeremias asks, regarding the quality of life and the joy of discovering the hidden treasure and the precious pearl, "What is the quality of a life which has been overmastered by this great joy? It is to follow Jesus. Its characteristic is the love whose pattern is to be found in the Lord who has become a servant …" (201). Therefore, the true worth of the Reign of God is not merely in the study of the word of God, as the rabbis believed, but it is determined by learning from Jesus how to be a servant. This is the ultimate expression of the Shema.

Up to this point, Jesus has emphasized qualities of the Kingdom that deal with obedience, faith, and internal dynamics that produce righteousness and judgment. These are the first parables to stress the worth of the Reign of God as a possession in the disciple's life. Its value is seen in a transformation that imitates Jesus.

Food for Thought

1. How would a Jew of the first century have interpreted the Parable of the Hidden Treasure and the Parable of the Precious Pearl?

2. What does Jesus add to the Jewish interpretation that makes the Reign of God personal?

3. How is the new concept of the Kingdom different from the Jewish concept?

4. Referring back to the guidelines of interpreting parables, which of these guidelines address the ethical question of the hidden treasure?

5. How is the true worth of the Kingdom determined?

6. What is the most meaningful thing you learned from this lesson?

Chapter 13

The Parable of the Dragnet

Matthew 13:47–50

The Parable of the Dragnet is a fishing story Jesus tells. Like most fishing stories we are used to hearing, this one uses familiar images from his day. But this fishing story is not about the one that got away. Instead, it is a story about the big catch. The parable reads as follows:

Once again, the Kingdom of heaven is like a net that was let down into the lake and caught all kinds of fish. When it was full, the fishermen pulled it up on the shore. Then they sat down and collected the good fish in baskets but threw the bad away. This is how it will be at the end of the age. The angels will come and separate the wicked from the righteous and throw them into the fiery furnace, where there will be weeping and gnashing of teeth.

Jewish Background

There were several ways of fishing commercially in Jesus' day. Seine-net fishing and cast-net fishing were common in ancient times and are still used in many places today. In seine-net fishing, a crew of fishermen, often in two boats, spread a large seine net across the water. The net was weighted to drag the bottom of the lake as it was pulled onto the shore or into the boat, catching everything that swam into it. This type of fishing was primarily done at night. Galilean fishermen were known to work all night, sometimes without catching anything (cf. Luke 5:3–6).

The parable tells of a catch consisting of *good* and *bad* fish. The Jewish dietary requirements, commanded in the Torah, forbade eating fish with no scales. The Book of Leviticus instructs, "But all creatures in the seas or streams that do not have fins and scales—whether among all the swarming things or all the other living creatures in the water—you are to detest. And since you are to detest them, you must not eat their meat, and you must detest their carcasses. Anything living in the water that does not have fins and scales is to be detestable to you" (Lev. 11:10–12). The Sea of Galilee is home to a fish similar to the American catfish. It is a scavenger fish that scours the bottom of the lake. Any species of fish, amphibian, or other aquatic creatures of this type were considered unclean by the Jews. The eating of their meat was an abomination to God. When Galilean fishermen netted a catch, they had the painstaking job of separating the fish. The good fish species were cleaned and salted for that day's market. The rest was thrown back into the sea or otherwise discarded.

Immediate Application to Jesus' Audience

Again, the setting has not changed from the preceding parables. Jesus spoke this parable while in the presence of his disciples. This parable parallels the Parable of the Weeds in the Field in many ways. He uses several of the same phrases and common images found in Jewish literature that we have already discussed from the Parable of the Weeds in the Field. A side-by-side comparison of their interpretations shows how the two parables are alike.

The Weeds in the Field	**The Dragnet**
The harvest is the end of the age.	This is how it will be at the end of the age, and the harvesters are angels.
The Son of Man will send out his angels and they will weed out of his kingdom everything that causes sin and all who do evil.	The angels will come and separate the wicked from the righteous …
They will throw them into the fiery furnace, where there will be weeping and gnashing of teeth.	and throw them into the fiery furnace, where there will be weeping and gnashing of teeth.

The key to understanding the Parable of the Dragnet is in the phrase *end of the age*. This identifies a timeframe. As with the Parable of the Weeds in the Field, this insists on fulfilling this prophetic parable within that generation. Once more, only Matthew used the phrase *end of the age*. The King James and 1901 American Standard versions translate *aionos* as "world." However, as Chapter Nine notes, *aionos* is a dispensation of time or an era. It does not mean the end of the *world* in a universal sense. In our study of the Parable of the Weeds in the Field, we concluded that the end of the age meant the end of the Jewish era with the destruction of the Temple and Jerusalem in A.D. 70. Therefore, the end of the age cannot refer to the end of time and be consistent with the context here and elsewhere in Matthew where the phrase is used.

The parable begins by saying, "The Kingdom of Heaven is like a net." This reference to the Kingdom clearly speaks of the multidimensional nature of the Reign of God through Christ, who rules over good and evil, righteous and wicked. In the multidimensional Kingdom of God, Jesus possesses the right to execute judgment with a rod of iron and justification with the scepter of righteousness.

We are again introduced to angelic activity as in the Parable of the Weeds in the Field. Most commentaries do not suggest an immediate fulfillment of this parable but place its fulfillment at the end of time with the Second Coming. It seems more correct to imply that upon the disciples' remembrance of Christ's prediction of the destruction of Jerusalem, these *angels*—who could be human messengers of God rather than heavenly beings—gathered his church and led them to a haven away from the destruction. Again, the Jewish-Christian congregation fled Jerusalem across the Jordan into the city of Pella before the Temple and Jerusalem were razed by the Romans. Once again, the language of judgment will be similar whether in the realm of time or at the end of time.

This interpretation excludes Gentile Christians. If my application of the parable is correct, Gentile Christians are *not* in view here. Instead, this parable addresses *only* Jewish Christians and what will happen at the end of the Jewish era. The "good" and the "bad" were separated by the judgment of the A.D. 70 destruction of Jerusalem. History bears this out as exactly what happened. Therefore, it is my conclusion that to suggest that the Parable of the Dragnet teaches about judgment at the end of time makes a giant leap without textual justification.

The Tragedy of Rejecting the Reign of God

The Parable of the Dragnet was spoken in connection with the twin parables of the Hidden Treasure and the Priceless Pearl. These are deliberately sandwiched between the interpretation of the Parable of the Weeds in the Field and the Parable of the Dragnet to underscore the tragedy of rejecting the immeasurable worth of the Reign of God through Christ in the disciple's life. It served as a warning of judgment for those who fail to believe in Jesus as their Messiah. This warning is no less true for us today. Anyone who chooses to reject Jesus as the Messiah will likewise be condemned.

I want to conclude this examination with the words of C. H. Dodd, which underscores this discussion. Dodd writes, "Let us then go back to the common underlying meaning of the expression 'Kingdom of God' in all its various uses. It means God exercising his kingly rule among men. In particular, it implies that the divine power is effectively at issue with the evil in the world. In this sense, judgment is a function of the Kingdom of God. In history, it brings the effective condemnation of sin" (56). The unbelieving Jews of Jesus' day had rejected the Reign of God, making the Divine Power effectively at issue with them.

This completes the overall message of the parables thus far in this context. The Jews, who rejected the message of the Reign of God, are characterized in the Parable of the Sower as the pathway and perhaps the rocky ground. They neglected their faith and were devoid of righteousness. These failed to find in Jesus the hidden treasure and the priceless pearl while they had the opportunity. They are the sons of the evil one, described as the bad fish according to the Parable of the Dragnet.

Summary

The Jews primarily viewed the Kingdom of Heaven as a place to enter or a future age heralding the arrival of Elijah and the Messiah. While it's true that the Kingdom of God is to be entered, these parables teach us that the Kingdom, or Reign of God, is multi-dimensional. His reign has always been present and powerful and must be internalized and personified in our imitation of Christ.

Food for Thought

1. What dietary law does this parable suggest?

2. Discuss the similarities between the Parable of the Weeds in the Field and the Dragnet.

3. Discuss again the significance of the *end of the age.*

4. How do the Parables of the Hidden Treasure and the Priceless Pearl fit into the parables of the Weeds in the Field and the Dragnet Net?

5. Summarize the overall message of the Kingdom Parables so far.

6. What is the most meaningful thing you learned from this lesson?

Chapter 14

The Parable of the House Owner

Matthew 13:51–52

This last parable in Matthew chapter 13 serves as a conclusion for this series of parables. It has been an eventful day for the disciples, filled with drama, apprehension, and instruction. As this school day at the feet of this unique Jewish rabbi draws to a close, Jesus asks them a question. "'Have you understood all these things?' ... 'Yes,' they replied. He said to them, 'Therefore every teacher of the law who has been instructed about the Kingdom of heaven is like the owner of a house who brings out of his storeroom new treasures as well as old.'"

Jewish Background

What might seem to us as a simple proverb was a parable, which was, to the disciples, a parable filled with familiar Jewish images. They do not capture our attention as easily. Here are the phrases that would have caught their attention.

The first one is about the *teacher of the law*. This is a Jewish scribe. Historically, the scribes were a class of well-educated Jewish men who specialized in the academics of the written Torah. Ezra was a scribe in the post-exilic period (Ezra 7:10). During ancient times, scribes were personal secretaries, such as Baruch, the prophet Jeremiah's secretary. They worked as secretaries for kings, secretaries of state, and business. During the time of Christ, scribes were public teachers from the Pharisaic sect, known for their ability to teach the Torah and the oral traditions of Judaism. They were also called lawyers in the New Testament, which can be somewhat confusing. They were the professors and scholars of their day. The scribe's primary purpose was to preserve the accuracy of God's word and its practice and teach the Torah to Israel.

Jesus acknowledged their ability to teach God's word but warned the disciples not to follow their ways (Matt. 23:13). The scribes believed that perfect adherence to the Law was possible and the pathway to justification. Consequently, they bound burdens on people and demanded flawless performance, teaching that this is the way of righteousness. As one might imagine, there was no room for grace in their dealings with people. Their loveless law-keeping ways caused them to meticulously count every commandment carefully for fear of leaving out a single one. Their count came to 613 commandments and laws.

While this well-intended pursuit of excellence is commendable, they failed to understand how the *Shema* and its twin commandment were intended to work. Simply being a commandment-keeper does not produce love for God and one's neighbor, as the *Shema* teaches. Instead, loving God, as the *Shema* teaches, with the whole heart, soul, mind, and strength—and loving one's neighbor as oneself—fulfills all of God's commandments. Their misguided view of this truth caused them to go even further by developing a safeguard system designed to protect the Torah from being violated. The scribes made themselves busy building "fences" around the commandments. Later, these became known as "Judah-hedges." These are the traditions Jesus vehemently condemned because they canceled out the commandments of God (Matt. 15:5–6).

The scribes and Pharisees thought they had a solution to the sin problem, not realizing the one they had created. According to their perverted remedy, an individual would have to break a series of traditions by mistake or out of ignorance before the commandment was broken. For example, they listed thirty-nine acts prohibited on the Sabbath to guard against breaking the fourth commandment. By observing these traditions, they believed that the Torah could be lived perfectly and hasten the coming of the Kingdom of God.

This is why, by the time of Christ, the scribes and Pharisees began determining a person's orthodoxy by his respect for the fences (Moseley 90–1). Should we really be looking to scribes as positive role models? It doesn't sound like it. Why, then, would Jesus commend a scribe in this parable? I will answer that question in a moment. Before we answer this question, let's consider the following Jewish phrase.

The following Jewish phrase in this parable, recognizable by the disciples, speaks of a teacher of the law being "instructed about the Kingdom of Heaven." Again, the phrase *Kingdom of Heaven* is a Jewish euphemism for God and his sovereign rule. The phrase we are interested in here is the word *instructed*. It means *to be made a disciple*. The New International Version's translation of this text leads us to understand that the scribe is instructed *about* the Kingdom of Heaven. This needs to be understood differently. It seems to be more than instructed *about* the Kingdom. While there are variations in the Greek text on this verse, the idea seems to be that the Reign of God is being brought *into* the disciple's life as a seed is planted into good soil. The Reign of God must be implanted. Of course, this is precisely what the Parable of the Sower implies. In ancient times, the disciple lived with his teacher. He studied his teacher as much as the Torah and its Mishnah (see Matt. 10:24–25). To be instructed about the Kingdom of Heaven meant that the Reign of God was brought into the disciple's life.

The last thing we want to consider is the house owner who "brings out of his storeroom treasures." His treasure is said to contain both "new and old." Conceivably, a family in the first century could have owned the same property that had been in the family since the return of the exiles from Babylon. Therefore, they might very well have treasured new and ancient things that they had inherited.

Application

The immediate application is intended for Jesus' disciples, but it is not limited to them. First, we must consider the question directed to Jesus' disciples. This parable hinges on this question: *"Have you understood all these things?"* It is difficult to imagine Jesus merely inquiring about their general comprehension of what he said. He appears to be asking whether they had grasped the meaning of what he had taught them. These Kingdom Parables were composed in such a way as to assist their understanding and help them comprehend the mysterious ways of the Reign of God. As parables do, they demanded a response. If not responded to appropriately, severe consequences were in store. They needed to understand the nature of the Reign of God and the kingdom person's response. In other words, these parables were presented as a test to determine their discipleship. Not only was Jesus revealing the mysteries of the multi-dimensional nature of the Reign of God, but he was sifting his listeners to reveal those who would become or continue to be his disciples. The parables were designed to draw the disciples into Jesus' inner circle while alienating his opponents even more.

This parable compares the disciple to a scribe, a teacher of the Torah, *discipled* into the Reign of God. I cannot imagine that Jesus intended to take every aspect of a first-century scribe and apply it to his disciples. The scribes at the time of Christ were characterized as *not* practicing what they preached. Instead, I believe he intended to apply the character of the ideal scribe, a diligent student of God's word, able to explain the Torah effectively and put it into daily practice like Ezra. When the qualities of the ideal scribe are combined with being discipled into the Reign of God, the result is a kingdom person who is equipped to teach and make disciples. This answers our previous question, asking why Jesus would commend a scribe in this parable. The ideal scribe is a good model for the kingdom person.

The parable also speaks of a treasure in which there are new and ancient things.

The Greek word *kaine* (pronounced kai-nay), translated as *new* in this passage, is interesting because it does not always mean "brand new" but is new to you. In many cases, it can refer to something *new to you*. We use the same expression when buying an older house, for example. It is old but *new to us*. However, it might not be "brand new." Similarly, the treasure of which Jesus speaks might seem new, but it is quite ancient. The Reign of God in the lives of his people bears this same quality in that it is simultaneously new and ancient.

This suggests that *Jesus is not revealing a new kingdom*. Occasionally, I will hear someone speak or read something someone has written on the subject of the Messianic Kingdom as if it is a new Kingdom rather than an eternal Kingdom being restored to Israel. (Refer to the Chapter 23 for a full discussion on this point). Perhaps the way Jesus reveals the Reign of God causes us to view it as something new. What was once a mystery is now being revealed in enlightening new ways—not as a new Kingdom. New things can be discovered from ancient things. The Book of Hebrews is a good illustration. The Hebrew writer outlines the new things found in Christ, yet he begins his letter by describing the eternal throne of the Christ. He then says, "Jesus is the same yesterday, today, and forever" (Heb. 1:8; 13:8). Therefore, the treasure is indeed new, yet it is ancient. Only eternal things can be spoken in these terms because they bear attributes of God. It bears the character of antiquity while never growing old.

A Parable of the Great Commission?

As we all know, with knowledge comes responsibility. When the Reign of God is brought into the disciple's life, he becomes like a householder with a treasure storeroom. We are reminded at this point of the Parables of the Hidden Treasure and the Pearl of Great Price that speak of the joy of discovery, the immeasurable value, and the preciousness of the Reign of God. We might also be reminded of Paul's words in 2 Cor. 4:7. Paul writes, "But we have this treasure in jars of clay to show that this all-surpassing power is from God and not from us." This "all-surpassing power" speaks of the demonstration of God's reign. The treasure is the message of the Reign of God in Christ. The jars of clay are disciples who are storehouses into which the Reign of God is placed.

The house owner is said to bring out treasure from his storeroom. This is a good example of how our English translations sometimes lack the expression of emotion that is in the original language. Pictured here is a man reaching into his treasure trove. With exuberance and enthusiasm, he tosses his treasure, sharing it with others. His giving expresses excitement.

What greater treasure is there than the Gospel of Christ? What greater privilege is there than sharing it? This parable appears to preview the Great Commission. Below is a comparison of the parable with Matthew's version of the Great Commission.

Matthew 13:52	Matthew 28:19
The scribe made a disciple.	Go, make disciples.
He is discipled into the Kingdom.	Baptizing into the name of the Father, Son, and Holy Spirit.

Matthew 13:52	Matthew 28:19
He brought out of his storeroom treasures, new anc ancient.	Teaching to observe all things I have commanded you.

From the above comparison, the scribe made a disciple is likened to being disciplined in Matthew 28:19. The disciple then responds to the Reign of God by being baptized into the name of the Father, Son, and Holy Spirit. Then, the disciple is trained to disciple others through his teaching of the Good News using concepts that are both new and old.

Now, for one final item, we must not overlook the moral obligation to share the treasure. This is subtly suggested if we consider that the treasure is an inheritance. An inheritance, by definition, is received by grace. A constant reminder of Jesus to his disciples that is echoed here seems to be, "Freely you have received, freely give" (Matt. 10:8). Paul certainly felt this moral obligation when he said, "Yet when I preach the gospel, I cannot boast, for I am compelled to preach. Woe to me if I do not preach the gospel!" (1 Cor. 9:16) Therefore, the message of this parable becomes a moral obligation, or to put it another way—a Kingdom assignment. The disciple trained in the Reign of God will enthusiastically be compelled to fulfill his obligation by sharing this new and ancient spiritual treasure with others.

Food for Thought

1. What is the significance of the *teacher of the law*?

2. Discuss how Jewish legalists approached the Law and its effect on their treatment of people.

3. Discuss the phrase in the NIV that reads, *instructed about the Kingdom of Heaven.* What is the correct interpretation?

4. What two meanings can be applied to the word *new* from the Greek word *kaine*?

5. Discuss the so-called "new kingdom" concept and explain how Jesus viewed the Kingdom from this parable.

6. How is this parable a preview of the Great Commission?

7. What is the most meaningful thing you learned from this lesson?

Part 3

Chapter 15

The Parable of the Merciful King, Part 1

Matthew 18:23–35

Most of us know this parable as the Parable of the Unmerciful Servant. In this study, it will be referred to as the Parable of the Merciful King. It is the actions of a merciful pagan king that Jesus is comparing to the Reign of God rather than the actions of the unmerciful servant. From this parable, we will learn that the greatest in the Kingdom of Heaven is the one who forgives from the heart. Here is the parable from Matthew 18:23–35:

> Therefore, the Kingdom of Heaven is like a king who wants to settle accounts with his servants. As he began the settlement, a man who owed him ten thousand talents was brought to him. Since he was not able to pay, the master ordered that he, his wife, his children, and all that he had be sold to repay the debt. The servant fell on his knees before him. "Be patient with me," he begged, "and I will pay back everything." The servant's master took pity on him, canceled the debt, and let him go. But when that servant went out, he found one of his fellow servants who owed him a hundred denarii. He grabbed him and began to choke him. "Pay back what you owe me!" he demanded. His fellow servant fell to his knees and begged him, "Be patient with me, and I will pay you back." But he refused. Instead, he had the man imprisoned until he could pay the debt. When the other servants saw what had happened, they were greatly distressed

and went and told their master everything that had happened. Then, the master called the servant in. "You wicked servant," he said, "I canceled all that debt of yours because you begged me to. Shouldn't you have had mercy on your fellow servant just as I had on you?" In anger, his master turned him over to the jailers to be tortured until he could pay back all he owed. This is how my heavenly Father will treat you unless you forgive your brother from your heart.

Cultural Background—Jewish or Gentile?

The king and his servants depicted in this parable fit the bureaucratic establishment within an agrarian society of the late Second Temple period. In other words, the king is an aristocrat or high-profile ruler who rose to the highest level of the political hierarchy, where bribery was the way to success. It was a corrupt society where the highest bidder was often appointed to office, and oppressively high taxation ensured a quick financial reimbursement. This makes the background of this parable more Gentile than Jewish. This was not the only time Jesus chose non-Jews to be role players in his parables to teach a fundamental truth about the Reign of God. For instance, Jesus chose a non-Jew in his Parable of the Good Samaritan. A despised Samaritan is used as an example for a Jewish lawyer to stress the practice of the *Shema* and its twin commandment (Luke 10:25–27).

While the Jews despised Samaritans more than they despised Gentiles, they viewed the Gentiles as ungodly, cruel, and brutal pagans. Nothing good was associated with the Gentile world, though a few individuals were considered exceptions to that rule. Consider Nathanael's response to hearing that the Prophet of whom Moses and the prophets spoke had come from Nazareth. "Nazareth!" he replied with a tone of disbelief. "Can anything good come from there?" (John 1:46) Nazareth of Galilee was adjacent to the Gentile regions and was infamous for its outlaws.

The Jewish estimation of Gentile rulers was no better. A pagan ruler in the Roman world typically was anything but good. So, highlighting a pagan ruler in a favorable light would have raised eyebrows. But in Jesus' typical fashion, he presents a culturally infused oxymoron to compel his disciples to be like God in their actions toward people. Paul used this same tactic when preaching the gospel to the Gentiles as a method of saving the Jews. He writes that preaching the same terms of the gospel to both Jews and Gentiles was "in the hope that I may somehow arouse my own people to envy and save some of them" (Rom. 11:14). As Paul provoked the Jews to consider the saving of the Gentiles, Jesus appears to be prodding his disciples to forgive the way God forgives through a parable about a merciful pagan king.

A bureaucratic ruler of the governing class in that society operated above the law and was amenable only to the authorities of Rome. His subordinates, especially the common people, fearfully respected his power and authority. His servants were court officials, tax collectors, and tribute retainers. They are called *servants* in the parable to contrast their subservient position to his. However, like the king, they are also aristocrats vying for power. As government offices were offered to the highest bidder, their ambition was to usurp the king by becoming wealthier and more powerful. The king's power and authority are only as secure as his ability to maintain them. This provides a political insider's look into a royal court where tax collectors are called to give an account of the ruler's finances.

The parable describes one servant as having a debt of ten thousand talents. A talent was six thousand denarii in their currency. One could argue that this excessive debt is absurd, even given taxes and tribute to be collected. We could assume Jesus is making use of hyperbole. However, Josephus recorded tributes of twenty thousand silver talents (Book 12, 4:1). The second debt of one hundred denarii was the yearly wage of a common laborer. So, it is reasonable that this parable represents a fair and realistic picture of a part of society that Matthew, a former tax collector, knew very well.

The servant had been embezzling tax money totaling ten thousand talents. The Roman government allowed them to tax the people as much as they wanted, as long as they paid their lords and Rome received its share. Consequently, many people were bankrupted and enslaved, while tax collectors enjoyed the good life of the upper echelon of society.

The language implies that he had been arrested because he was "brought" before the king. Picturing pagan tax collectors being summoned to give an account to their lords must have brought smiles, at first, to the faces of Jesus' disciples. Gentile tax collectors were hated, while Jewish tax collectors were hated even more. They were considered traitors of Israel and called Roman lovers. The Jewish rabbis believed that tax collectors were just as disreputable as prostitutes. Priests even refused to accept their tithes and sacrifices of worship at the Temple. The teaching of the Mishnah made it "lawful" to cheat tax collectors (Nedarim 27b; 28a). It encouraged people to be fraudulent taxpayers, making corrupt tax collectors more corrupt and oppressive.

The sentence for his crime was slavery, together with his wife, children, and property. This is our first suspicion that the king and his servants are Gentiles. Jeremias (211) writes, "Jewish law only permitted the sale of an Israelite in case of theft, if the thief could not restore what he had stolen; the sale of a wife was forbidden under Jewish jurisdiction."

There are several references to tax collectors in the Gospels. For example, we see that tax collectors were like everyone else. They needed forgiveness, and some sought it. Tax collectors came to be baptized by John and were instructed to practice kingdom ethics by not collecting more than was required (Luke 3:12–13). Matthew, one of the disciples, was a tax collector who left his tax booth to follow Jesus (Matt. 10:3). Zacchaeus was a wealthy chief tax collector who sought Jesus and prepared a banquet for which Jesus was his honored guest (Luke 9:2). In another example, Jesus reflects the Jewish disdain for tax collectors by saying that a disciple who refuses to repent should be treated as a pagan and a tax collector (Matt. 18:17). Jesus did not share this Jewish contempt but used it as a teaching point regarding discipline. Jesus also spoke a parable about a tax collector and a Pharisee who went to the Temple to pray. The tax collector went home forgiven, while the Pharisee was not forgiven (Luke 18:10–14). Jesus angered the Pharisees by saying tax collectors and prostitutes were entering God's reign ahead of them (Matt. 21:31).

The Context

Space will not allow us to insert the full text. Please take a moment to read Matthew 18:1–5 with Mark 9:37–41 to complete the text. Follow this reading with Matthew 18:6–9 adding Mark 9:47–50. Finally, read Matthew 18:10–35. As you read, note that the Kingdom is mentioned four times in this context (Matt. 18:1, 4, 23; Mark 9:47), indicating that the whole discourse is about the activity of the Reign of God and how we are expected to imitate that activity.

Jesus spoke this parable in the presence of the twelve disciples and several others in the house. He often traveled with a sizable group of men, women, and children. He told this parable while they were in Galilee, just before making his way to Jerusalem to celebrate the Jewish Feast of Tabernacles (see John 7:1–9). The parable comes directly from a context that contains two questions—both of which influence this parable. Here are the two questions:

1. The disciples asked, "Who is the greatest in the Kingdom of heaven?" (Matt. 18:1; Mark 9:33b–34; Luke 9:46.)
2. Peter asked, "Lord, how many times should I forgive my brother when he sins against me? Up to seven times?" (Matt. 18:21)

The first question about who the greatest in the Kingdom is will not be the last time this will be addressed. Later, the mother of the Zebedee brothers will come to Jesus and ask that her sons be given prominent positions in the Messianic Kingdom (Matt. 20:20; Mark 10:35–45.). After all, vying for position was the way to greatness in their society.

Jesus answered their question about who the greatest is by placing a young boy before them. This child represented a disciple of the Messiah, a brother, and a child of the Kingdom, emphasizing the necessity of humility. Anything more only creates the likelihood that the *little one* could be sinned against. Welcoming or receiving a disciple as a kingdom person requires the attitude and spirit of acceptance where justification is practiced. This ensures treatment with dignity and acceptance with unconditional love that honors Christ. To cause someone to sin or to mistreat them is an expression of hatred. What a tragedy it is when someone is mistreated in the name of Christ. Jesus gives a stern warning for causing one of his disciples to stumble.

The parallel passage from Mark's account follows Matthew 18:9 with a quote from Isaiah 66:24. Mark then adds this saying of Jesus, *"Everyone will be salted with fire. Salt is good, but if it loses its saltiness, how can you make it salty again? Have salt in yourselves, and be at peace with each other."* This reference to salt in Mark's narrative of this discourse is no small detail. It has within it something that ties it to redemptive relationships. If you were to ask the average Bible class about the use of salt, most would respond by saying that salt was used as a preservative, and that is what it represents. The teacher usually will complement their answer by making an application to the Christian's good life. While it is true that we are to preserve the pursuit of holiness and righteousness on the earth, this is not an accurate application of salt from the Torah and Jewish teaching, nor is it what Jesus intended to communicate. This application has very little biblical basis at all. To simply say that salt is a metaphor for preservation is a misapplication. Perhaps one could argue that it refers to the *everlasting* quality of that which is in view, but salt is more than an agent in Scripture. It is a symbol that has a covenant-making connection associated with it.

Salt was used in ancient Jewish times in various ways, from lining the floors of ovens to medicinal uses to flavoring and food preservation. But salt was one of the ingredients commanded in the Torah to be added to the sacrifices, the making of showbread, and incense. *The Jewish Encyclopedia* notes that: "Just as none of the sacrifices could be offered without priests, so they could not be offered without salt."[13] This ingredient is called in the Torah the *salt of the covenant*. Notice the association of salt with covenant-keeping in the following Scriptures. The following emphasis is mine.

- "Season all your grain offerings with salt. Do not leave the **salt of the covenant** of your God out of your grain offerings; add salt to all your offerings." (Lev. 2:13)
- "Whatever is set aside from the holy offerings the Israelites present to the LORD I give to you and your sons and daughters as your regular share. It is an everlasting **covenant of salt** before the LORD for both you and your offspring." (Num. 18:19)

- "Don't you know that the LORD, the God of Israel, has given the kingship of Israel to David and his descendants forever by a **covenant of salt**"? (2 Chron. 13:5)

Therefore, the Torah's teaching on salt symbolizes God's everlasting covenant with his people—emphasizing salt concerning the covenant. This would have been something the Jewish ear in Jesus' day would *not* have missed. It would have grabbed their attention. This might explain the apparent interpolation—an adding of text by a scribe—into Mark 9:49, which made its way into the King James Version. This interpolation reads, "For everyone shall be salted with fire, and every sacrifice shall be salted with salt." While transcribing the Gospel of Mark, a Jewish-Christian scribe interpreted this passage as being about sacrifices offered on the altar and added this inscription. As time passed, what might have begun as a marginal note found its way into the text of later manuscripts.

Sacrifice, fire, salt, and covenant are all elements associated with the redemptive relationship between God and his people, where peace is enjoyed. For this reason, ancient Israelites shared salt with bread at the table to solidify and celebrate their friendships. Even today, Arab nomads in the Middle East have an expression that says, "There is salt between us." This is to say, there is a covenant of friendship between the two. Salt is a metaphor for the ingredient necessary for redemptive relationships. It represents a covenant. Therefore, Jesus says, *"Have salt in yourselves and be at peace with each other."* (Mark 9:50)

Food for Thought

1. How can we know that the background of this parable is Gentile rather than Jewish?

2. What is the apparent occupation of the king and his servants?

3. What are the two questions in the context that set up the parable?

4. Mark's account adds this statement of Jesus. *"Everyone will be salted with fire. Salt is good, but if it loses its saltiness, how can you make it salty again? Have salt in yourselves and be at peace with each other."* Discuss the significance of salt in biblical terms.

5. What has *salt* to do with forgiveness?

6. What is the most meaningful thing you learned from this lesson?

Chapter 14

The Parable of the Merciful King, Part 2

Matthew 18:23–35

The Application

In response to the disciples' question, "Who, then, is the greatest in the Kingdom of heaven?" Jesus follows with a discussion on pursuing peace with a brother when sin is involved (Matt. 18:1). This, then, brings us to the second question in the context. Peter asked, "Lord, how many times should I forgive my brother when he sins against me? Up to seven times?" (v. 21) Jesus responded, "I tell you, not seven times, but seventy-seven times." Peter was speaking out of his Jewish upbringing. The rabbis taught extensively about forgiveness, but it was to be limited to three offenses (Matt. 5:20). Rabbi Yose ben Hanina said, "He who asks forgiveness from his neighbor should not do so more than three times" (Mishnah, *Yoma,* 87a.). Rabbi Yose ben Yehuda taught, "If a person commits one offense, they forgive him; if he commits a second offense, they forgive him; if he offends a third time, they forgive him, but the fourth time, they do not forgive." They taught that there was no obligation to forgive beyond three times. Many of the Pharisees placed this kind of restriction on righteousness, which Jesus said we are to exceed to enter the Reign of God (Matt. 5:20). They legitimized their brand of forgiveness through necessary inference from passages like Amos 1:3 and Genesis 50:17. God said, *"for three transgressions and for four"* (Amos 1:3, 6, 9, 11, 13).They assumed that God would forgive three times, maybe four, but no more. From this misuse of Scripture and abuse of necessary inference, they reasoned that to forgive more than three, or at best four times, exceeded God's grace. You might say it was the Jewish version of three strikes and you're out.

Here, Jesus is seen intentionally challenging these rabbinic teachings to bring the disciples back to the original intent of the Torah regarding forgiveness and to teach how the Reign of God is demonstrated. Peter did not realize that to place a limit on forgiveness—even if it exceeded Jewish tradition—was tantamount to not forgiving at all. Peter's "grace system" was nothing more than a record-keeping system. This runs counter to forgiveness according to Jesus' grace system, which is not subject to record-keeping. In 1 Corinthians 13, Paul discusses love's demand well. In v. 5, we read that love *keeps no record of wrongs.* By rabbinic standards, this would have been too radical. Yet David writes, "Yes, what joy for those whose record the LORD has cleared of sin" (Psalm 32:2 NLT). This clearing of sin's record, which he celebrates, is the kind of forgiveness Jesus teaches as a Kingdom-kind of forgiveness. In other words, those living by the Reign of God do not have their sins recorded against them, nor do they keep a record of the sins of others.

Forgiveness is a Risky Business

Most of us do not like taking risks. We avoid them if we can, especially if the risk involves relationships. Some of us have tried to remove the risks, only to learn that we have caused more harm and hurt. When it comes to forgiveness, any attempt to withhold or set limitations upon forgiveness creates risks of its own. We need to realize that there will always be risks involved with forgiveness. There is no getting around it. The only way to prevent risks is to withhold forgiveness.

One of the risks is the willingness to respect the person being forgiven, while expecting that they will act irresponsibly with your forgiveness. Anything more or less is as mistreatment, unloving, and unforgiving. But what if the one we have forgiven has not acted responsibly with our forgiveness? What should I do if I am sinned against over and over? Or what if the person I have forgiven is like the servant in this parable who refuses to forgive others after he has been forgiven? Should our forgiveness be conditional, granted only if the recipient acts responsibly?

The merciful king took a tremendous risk by investing undeserved grace and trust to a disloyal servant, expecting him to be responsible with his pardon. Yet, the king was willing to take that risk. Perhaps he was counting on his grace to win the servant's loyalty in the form of repentance. Unfortunately, the servant did not act any more responsibly with his justification than he did when he embezzled his master's money. Sadly, the king took an incredible risk only to have his good favor mocked by his servant's refusal to do the same. It appears that everyone involved lost something. We may rightly ask—was it worth it? Perhaps this is part of what Jesus wants us to see. The tragedy of being unforgiving is that everyone involved loses. No one wins when we refuse to forgive.

We do not often think of God taking risks. Yet, the Parable of the Merciful King shows us that even God takes risks. Perhaps we are reluctant, or even dismissive, of this thought because risk-taking seems too human to be associated with God. By definition, it implies the inability to know what will happen. Some would even call it a gamble. God, however, is not a gambler because he knows what will happen. So, how can it be said that God's forgiveness involves the taking of risks?

Consider the risk he took when Jesus emptied himself to become human. There is something about the incarnation of Jesus that involved an enormous risk. The incarnation of Jesus required that he set aside all expressions of his deity while remaining fully God (Phil. 2:6–7; Col. 2:9.). This left him vulnerable to our vulnerabilities. Some have difficulty accepting this, believing that even though he was human, he couldn't sin because he was God. After all, he was God in the flesh. What purpose did it serve for him to struggle with temptation if no risk factor was involved? (Matt. 4:8–9) Jesus did not sin, but had Jesus fallen, as the first Adam did, no other option was available for us to be saved. There was only one chance. He was and is our only hope for redemption. There was no backup plan. The risk factor involved in choosing a cross was immense. When we hear him praying in the garden, "Father, if it is possible, may this cup pass from me," we hear his painful cry to remove the risk factor of the crucifixion. There was no question in the Father's mind about how well Jesus would do under the world's weight, but there were moments when God, as the Son of Man, felt the immense risk he was taking with every breath. Our debt is cleared because God was willing to take the risk at the expense of subjecting his Son to temptation and the humiliation of crucifixion.

From this, we learn that forgiveness involves taking God-sized risks. What will we do with the risks God has taken? As painful as it may be, the risk factor must remain part of the forgiveness process. Otherwise, we become like Peter, who at the time wanted to remove the risks so that eventually, our obligation to forgive is removed as well.

Forgiveness, the Shema, and Its Twin Commandment

I want to take a moment to examine how the *Shema's* twin commandment, to love your neighbor as yourself, is interwoven into this parable (Mark 12:31). This commandment sums up all the commandments because love is the fulfillment of the Torah, as Paul says in Romans 13:10. Notice again how Paul makes the connection in Colossians 3:13–15. The New Living Translation reads, "You must make allowances for each other's faults and forgive the person who offends you. Remember, the Lord forgave you, so you must forgive others. And the most important piece of clothing you must wear is love. Love is what binds us all together in perfect harmony. And let the peace that comes from Christ rule in your hearts. As members of one body, you are all called to live in peace." That familiar ring you should be hearing in this passage echoes the essence of the *Shema* and is strengthened by the new commandment of John 3:34. This ancient love mandate of Israel is the heart of forgiveness. It determines how well the Reign of God is demonstrated in our lives.

Very often, we struggle to forgive. Keeping the past in the past seems impossible when we have been betrayed and hurt. Even if forgiveness has to be renewed daily, the Reign of God in us should provide the strength we need today, which is sufficient. Paul said in Philippians 4:6, "Do not be anxious about anything, but in every situation, by prayer and petition, with thanksgiving, present your requests to God. And the peace of God, which transcends all understanding, will guard your hearts and your minds in Christ Jesus."

If you are struggling to entrust your forgiveness to someone who has caused you great pain or abused the grace you offered, tell it to God. He has experienced the abuse of his grace many times. He will take your burden and give you peace, allowing you to demonstrate his reign in your life through the power of forgiveness. The risk is worth it.

Conclusion

As Jesus often does with his parables, he carries his disciples beyond familiar experiences to imagine the unimaginable. In this section, a pagan king did the unthinkable by canceling his servant's enormous debt and clearing all charges against him. This was no acquittal. He was justified and treated as if he had not committed the crime. The king, representing the law, had the authority to enslave his servant. The law has no obligation to forgive the debt and drop the charges. However, this pagan king chose not to act according to the law. Instead, he took the risk, and he chose to act by grace.

The pagan king's great act of forgiveness was intended to create other great acts of forgiveness throughout his realm. But when the servant refused to act upon the king's grace, he failed to understand something significant. His king's reign would have been demonstrated through him by spreading this grace to others.

The same holds true for us. In human relationships, forgiveness is intended to be a reciprocating act that begins with God. When we fail to extend God's grace toward others, we refuse to demonstrate God's reign within us. Consequently, the servant's debt was reinstated, and he was imprisoned. Jesus said, "This is how my Father will treat you unless you forgive your brother from your heart" (Matt. 18:35).

Finally, greatness in the Kingdom of Heaven is measured by redemptive acts that come at a price. From the parable, Jesus communicates with vivid clarity the immeasurable grace of God and what the kingdom person's response should be. What stands out the most is the risk factor that forgiveness requires and how the Reign of God is fundamentally joined. Jesus illustrates in a dramatic way that removing the risk impedes our ability to forgive the way God forgives. It holds forgiveness at ransom, thereby making prisoners of our brothers or, at the very least, second-class citizens of the kingdom. This is why God's reign is never more powerfully demonstrated than when we take the risk to forgive as we have been forgiven and set our offender free.

Food for Thought

1. Discuss Peter's question about how often forgiveness should be given. Compare the rabbinic teaching of forgiveness and Peter's statement.

2. Discuss the risk the merciful king takes when he forgives his servant.

3. How does forgiveness involve risks?

4. Discuss how the Reign of God suffers when we refuse to forgive.

5. Discuss the relationship of the Reign of God, the *Shema*, and its twin commandment with forgiveness.

6. What is the most meaningful thing you learned from this lesson?

Chapter 17

The Parable of the Workers in the Vineyard

Matthew 20:1–16

It was common in ancient times for laborers to go to the marketplace, a kind of unemployment office. Some gathered for the gossip, while others wanted to find work. The parable does not say so, but the landowner's apparent urgency indicates the season of harvest. As a boy, I recall working on the farm from dawn to well past sunset during the planting and harvesting seasons. There was a sense of urgency because of two factors out of our control—the changing weather and the risk of crops ruining in the field. Like this landowner, we were on a mission. My father had the benefit of having three sons and one full-time employee. During the growing season, this was sufficient. However, when the time came to gather the crops in the barns, he hired extra help. He was always very generous. It was common for him to pay more than the average wage for farm work. He paid his full-time employee the same salary as his sons—including benefits. Some neighboring farmers thought this was foolish, but my father saw it as doing what was right. There was one thing he expected, however. When the hired help accepted his employment, it was understood they would work with the same urgency as the rest of us. Just as in this parable, the idleness of the marketplace was not to be transferred to the field.

Here is the parable:

> For the Kingdom of heaven is like a landowner who went out early in the morning to hire men to work in his vineyard. He agreed to pay them a denarius for the day and sent them into his vineyard. About the third hour, he went out and saw others

standing in the marketplace doing nothing. He told them, "You also go and work in my vineyard, and I will pay you whatever is right." So they went. He went out again about the sixth hour and the ninth hour and did the same thing. About the eleventh hour he went out and found still others standing around. He asked them, "Why have you been standing here all day long doing nothing?" "Because no one has hired us," they answered. He said to them, "You also go and work in my vineyard." When evening came, the owner of the vineyard said to his foreman, "Call the workers and pay them their wages, beginning with the last ones hired and going on to the first." The workers who were hired about the eleventh hour came and each received a denarius. So when those came who were hired first, they expected to receive more. But each one of them also received a denarius. When they received it, they began to grumble against the landowner. "These men who were hired last worked only one hour," they said, "and you have made them equal to us who have borne the burden of the work and the heat of the day." But he answered one of them, "Friend, I am not being unfair to you. Didn't you agree to work for a denarius? Take your pay and go. I want to give the man who was hired last the same as I gave you. Don't I have the right to do what I want with my own money? Or are you envious because I am generous?" So the last will be first, and the first will be last.

Jewish Background

The average daily wage for a commoner in Jesus' day was a denarius. This was considered sufficient to sustain a peasant worker and his family at a meager level. It was a life of poverty. Living from hand-to-mouth was a way of life for the average village peasant. The Talmud[14] says Rabbi Hillel lived in poverty on half of a denarius per day.

According to Jewish law, a worker had to be paid at the end of the day and according to the amount of work he had done (Lev. 19:13). However, the employer was not limited to the commandments of the Law. In other words, he was free to go beyond the Law, as we see this landowner doing. The Torah's legislation was only the minimum requirement. The twin commandment to the *Shema* permitted the Torah to be exceeded.

Contrary to what we often hear about Jewish life under the Torah, the Jewish people understood that charity and generosity were not intended to be restricted by the Law's demand. Therefore, this landlord's generosity would not have been completely unusual. He did what he was commanded and exceeded it. He considered his generosity to be *right*. I find it interesting that Jesus used this word to describe the actions of the landowner. The Greek word translated as *right* is *dikaios* (v.4), which has a connection in Judaism that is a God-like quality. As a character trait, it speaks of a person who has God's conscience and does what he believes is what God would do.

Application

Typically, when we study this parable, we question the fairness of the landowner because we fail to understand how law and grace can work together. The concept of grace was nothing new in the Jewish view of God's dealings with his people. To suggest that the Jews knew very little about the grace of God is a regrettable misreading of the Old Testament.[15] Therefore, this is not a parable intended to contrast the message of grace in Christianity against Pharisaic legalism, nor is it a parable teaching how God rewards his servants. Instead, it is simply a glimpse into God's inexplicable grace, as it has always been.

God's grace is only a part of the overall picture. As with the king in the Parable of the Merciful King, forgiving his servant's enormous debt was an expression of his reign. God's grace is an expression of his reign. This leads me to believe that the main point in the Parable of the Workers in the Vineyard is about the Reign of God and his right to do as he pleases (cf. Psalm 115:3). The fact that it pleases him to be gracious, beyond what we think is fair, is the very thing that demonstrates his sovereignty. God does not have to ask anyone permission to bestow grace. So, in the closing statement, Jesus makes it clear: *"So the last will be first, and the first last,"* simply because that is what he chooses.

Called By God's Grace

This is especially true when we consider the landowner's *calling*. The context from which this parable is given is seen in the discourse between the rich young ruler and Jesus. He came to Jesus seeking something that he wanted to secure. Jesus' response to the young man's question about keeping the commandments was not that unusual. However, he asked Jesus to be more specific since he did not consider his observance of the commandments to be the issue. When Jesus listed five of the last six of the Ten Commandments, the one that was not listed was, "You shall not covet." Covetousness is symptomatic of a failure to internalize the *Shema*. It was the observance of this commandment that was lacking in this man's spiritual life and the very thing that was robbing him of eternal life if left uncorrected. When Jesus tested his devotion to the tenth commandment, the young man went away, sorrowful, because he could not see himself giving all his possessions to the poor and being left in poverty. His covetousness made it impossible to answer the call of grace.

The rich young ruler stands in contrast to the workers in the parable, who were hired from the marketplace. These two reactions are combined to expose a flaw in the disciples' attitudes. Peter felt compelled to point out that they had left everything to follow Jesus. "What then will there be for us?" Peter asked. Jesus responded by revealing the roles of the twelve disciples in the Messianic Kingdom. Peter and the other disciples must have felt justified with the answer. However, what came next must have shocked them. Jesus revealed that, regardless of whether you are one of the enthroned twelve or simply one of his eleventh-hour followers, the reward is the same—eternal life.

Therefore, all demands of personal rights and accusations of unfairness are baseless because of grace. This made Peter's boast of leaving everything to follow Jesus (after seeing the rich young ruler walk away) pointless. How much we give up or think we have lost to follow Jesus does not matter. Willingness to forsake everything to answer the call of grace is what matters.

Conclusion

Although it might be an appropriate application to note that eleventh-hour disciples will receive the same as the first, this parable is not intended to teach how God rewards his servants. Instead, this parable teaches how God has always dealt with his people. It is a relationship that begins with grace and continues with our response to it. Jesus' disciples must understand that leaving everything to follow Jesus does not earn his favor.

Perhaps this parable demonstrates how commandment-keeping and grace should work together to do what is *right*. The one with a God-like character views God's commandment through grace rather than believing that grace cancels the commandment. Grace, illustrated by the landowner, fulfills the law through love. This is what the Reign of God is like.

Food for Thought

1. What did the Law require of employers toward their employees?

2. What did the commandment to love your neighbor as yourself permit?

3. The landowner did what was "right." Discuss what this meant in kingdom-ethical terms.

4. What is the main point of this parable?

5. How is the Reign of God like the landowner?

6. Discuss the significance of grace from this parable as an expression of the Reign of God.

7. Explain how law and grace work together and how grace fulfills the Law.

8. What is the most meaningful thing you learned from this lesson?

Chapter 18

The Parable of the Royal Wedding Banquet, Part One

Matthew 22:1–14

Good food and joyous occasions bring people together to celebrate life. God is a feast-making God, which shows how much he enjoys fellowship. Celebrating life is what God loves to do with those he loves and who love him.

This parable expresses this divine desire to celebrate life. Here is the Parable of the Royal Wedding Banquet in two parts:

PART ONE
Matthew 22:1–14
"Jesus spoke to them again in parables, saying: The Kingdom of heaven is like a king who prepared a wedding banquet for his son. He sent his servants to those who had been invited to the banquet to tell them to come, but they refused to come. Then he sent some more servants and said, 'Tell those who have been invited that I have prepared my dinner: My oxen and fattened cattle have been butchered, and everything is ready. Come to the wedding banquet.' But they paid no attention and went off—one to his field, another to his business. The rest seized his servants, mistreated them and killed them. The king was enraged. He sent his army and destroyed those murderers and burned their city. Then he said to his servants, 'The wedding banquet is ready, but those I invited did not deserve to come. Go to the street corners

and invite to the banquet anyone you find.' So the servants went out into the streets and gathered all the people they could find, both good and bad, and the wedding hall was filled with guests."

PART TWO

"But when the king came in to see the guests, he noticed a man there who was not wearing wedding clothes. 'Friend,' he asked, 'how did you get in here without wedding clothes?' The man was speechless. Then the king told the attendants, 'Tie him hand and foot, and throw him outside, into the darkness, where there will be weeping and gnashing of teeth.' For many are invited, but few are chosen."

Jewish Background

This parable and its context are filled with so much Jewish tradition that we will discuss its Jewishness throughout this chapter. A village wedding was regarded almost as highly as Yom Kippur—the Great Day of Atonement. This remains true of Jewish tradition today. Only a few things have changed over the centuries. It was a community-wide event welcoming the beginning of a new life for the bride and groom, marking the end of the betrothal. They were treated like royalty. Therefore, the wedding banquet was called a *Royal Feast* in ancient times. Two sets of invitations were sent. The first announced the wedding ceremony but did not provide a time or day. The second invitation called everyone together, announcing that everything was ready. This was typical of a wedding in a Jewish village.

However, this parable does not introduce a typical village wedding. The father is a king, not a commoner. Royal weddings followed many of the same customs, but as one might expect, they were much more elaborate. The guests included those of the upper class. At a royal wedding in Judea, you could expect to see the royal family, the High Priest and his family, the chief priests with members of their families, the leaders of the various sects of the Sadducees and Pharisees, and wealthy businessmen. It was not uncommon for a king to provide expensive garments for the guests as they arrived. Each guest was expected to wear it since it proved they had been invited to the wedding. It was unthinkable and insulting to the host to refuse to wear the wedding garment, much less enter the wedding hall without it.

Two rabbinic parables contain remarkable similarities. One is attributed to Rabbi Johanan ben Zakkai, and it bears the most resemblance. It's recorded in the Babylonian Talmud (*Shabbat,* 153a). Its context is about repentance and keeping one's garments white, knowing that death could come at any moment. The rabbis taught that each person's goal should be to return one's spirit to God as pure as it was when given (*Shabbat,* 152b). Those who kept their garments pure were welcomed to the banquet table, while those who did not were placed outside. R. Johanan ben Zakkai said:

> This may be compared to a king who summoned his servants to a banquet without appointing a time. The wise ones adorned themselves and sat at the door of the palace. ["for,"] said they "is anything lacking in a royal palace? The fools went about their work, saying, 'can there be a banquet without preparations?" Suddenly, the king desired [the presence of] his servants: the wise entered adorned, while the fools entered soiled. The king rejoiced at the wise but was angry with the fools. "Those who adorned themselves for the banquet," ordered he, "let them sit, eat and drink. But those who did not adorn themselves for the banquet, let them stand and watch." (*Shabbat,* 153a)

Both Jesus and Rabbi Johanan spoke of a king, the inviting of guests, garments, and a banquet. In Jewish terms, these were symbols of the age to come and were associated with the reign of the Messiah. Israel's hope included seated with Abraham, Isaac, and Jacob at the banquet table in the Kingdom of God. "Blessed is the man who will eat at the feast of the Kingdom of God," one exclaimed (Luke 14:15).

The Context and Audience

Of course, the context of this parable is essential to understanding its purpose. It is rich with spiritual implications. The Parable of the Royal Wedding Banquet is the last in a quick series of three parables. Starting at the beginning of Matthew's narrative, chapter 21 begins with Jesus leaving Bethany and marking the first day of the Passion Week (see John 12:11–12). He approached Jerusalem riding on a donkey colt in a triumphal procession, evoking the Messianic passage of Zechariah 9:9.

As he approached Jerusalem, he was overcome with emotion, saying, "If you, even you, had only known on this day what would bring you peace, but now it is hidden from your eyes. The days will come upon you when your enemies will build an embankment against you and encircle you and hem you in on every side. They will dash you to the ground, you and the children within your walls. They will not leave one stone on another because you did not recognize the time of God's coming to you" (Luke 19:42–44). This is the prologue for four Messianic acts performed by Jesus under the very noses of members of the Sanhedrin.

ACT ONE

As for his first Messianic act, Jesus entered Jerusalem as the *Son of David* and went straight to the Temple as the Messiah was expected to do. The phrase *Son of David* has always been a title used to refer to the coming Messiah, the King of Israel. There was also a connection between the *Son of David* and the *Prophet*—the Second Moses of Deuteronomy 18:15. After heralding the arrival of the Son of David by the crowds and upon entering Jerusalem, when asked who Jesus was, the crowds answered, "This is Jesus, the prophet from Nazareth in Galilee" (Matt. 21:11). Their reply was not just that he was *a* prophet, but *the Prophet*—the Second Moses. Both titles, *Son of David* and the *Prophet*, have *Redeemer* associated with them. Next, we read that it was late in the day by this time. So, he and the twelve traveled back to Bethany for the night (Mark 11:11). This completes his first Messianic act of the week.

ACT TWO

On the second day, Jesus left Bethany early in the morning. On the way, hungry, he approached a fig tree to find figs to eat. But because it had none, he destroyed it by pronouncing it accursed. Upon entering Jerusalem again, he stormed into the Temple courtyard, turning over the tables of the moneychangers (Matt. 21:18–19; 12:12ff; Mark 11:12ff; Luke 19:45ff.). This was his second Messianic act in as many days. He gained the people's attention the day before with his triumphal entry. On this day, he attracted the people's attention by enforcing his Messianic authority, saying, "My house will be called a house of prayer for all nations" (Mark 11:17), quoting parts of Isaiah 56:7 and Jeremiah 7:11.

Annas, the High Priest, had established a lucrative business from the Temple. His moneychangers were in the currency exchange business. Foreign monies were illegal to use for Temple services. Livestock and doves for sacrifices were exchanged and sold at a hefty profit. As conditions would have it, the courtyard was noisy with the sound of a marketplace and the smell of a stock barn.

To make matters worse, these booths and livestock pens were set up in the court of the Gentiles, where foreign worshipers gathered. In Jesus' day, Gentile worshipers had become objects for many of the Jewish leaders to exploit rather than souls to reach. As a result, the Gentile-seekers of God were being dishonored.

By removing the extortionists from the court of the Gentiles, Jesus swept his Father's house clean of the leaven that defiled. Not surprisingly, this display of authority gained the attention of the Gentile worshipers. After this incident, we read in John 12:20-21 that some Greeks came to Philip asking to see Jesus. In response to their request, Jesus speaks of his mission in a summary statement. "But I, when I am lifted up from the earth, will draw all men to myself" (John 12:32). The time for the Gentiles to be called and invited to be God's people had arrived.

The religious establishment had caused God's missionary purpose to become lost in their covetousness and loveless law-keeping. They had forgotten their ancient God-given responsibility to be a light to the nations. The shepherds had turned inward and became self-absorbed in their self-righteousness. This gave greater significance to Jesus' use of Isaiah 56:7b, which reads, "for **my house** will be called a house of prayer **for all the nations**" (emphasis mine).

Before getting into the implication of his use of Isaiah and how it relates to his actions, I want to call our attention to chapter two of the Gospel of John, where Jesus cleansed the Temple the first time. Both cleansings occur before a Passover and a Feast of Unleavened Bread, which is noteworthy. According to the Torah, anything containing yeast was to be removed from the homes of Israel on the first day of the feast week (Exo. 12:15). There is a connection between Jesus' cleansing of the Temple and the preparation of the Passover.

Jesus entered his Father's house and cleansed it of its "leaven," driving it out. Jesus found that his Father's house had not been swept clean of corruption. Consequently, his Father's house was defiled, and God's typological purpose for it was defiled, thus distorting its symbolism. As in the days of Jeremiah before the first destruction, they had made it a "den of robbers." Someone has said that the difference between a thief and a robber is that a thief breaks in and steals, but a robber breaks in and commits violence. The Jewish elite were guilty of defiance, particularly regarding the *Shema*. This flouting of God's commandment resulted in the violent act of sinning against their neighbor—in this case, the Gentiles (Westermann 61–2). The Jewish elite had once again made the Temple a "den of robbers." Anytime God's people fail to fulfill his assignment to the world, we are guilty of committing violence to God's mission and to those he is seeking to save. Jesus did not approve of their neglect then, and he certainly does not approve of ours today.

My House Is a House of Prayer

Now we are ready for the significance of Jesus' use of Isaiah 56:7b. As we have seen already in chapter two, *Approaching the Sacred Text,* the ancient Jewish method of interpreting the Hebrew Scriptures is quite complicated, to say the least. During the late Second Temple period, the Bible wasn't divided into chapters and verses as we have today. The ancient Jewish use of the Hebrew Bible was to study and memorize the scriptures with its *midrashim* (rabbinic interpretation) in sections or units. Within these units of scripture, key phrases were used to identify a passage. Whenever a phrase was quoted, it would not only bring to mind a particular passage but also recall the whole unit's content and message. This is what Jesus was doing when he quoted what we now know as Isaiah 56:7b. By quoting this passage, his listeners could recall the overall message. It was immediately understood as applying to the present situation.

What was the message? First, Isaiah 56 is a message assuring God's acceptance of foreigners and eunuchs who chose to return with the Jews from Babylonian captivity. They would have been the most discouraged because, according to a strict adherence to the Torah, they would have been denied fellowship with God's people and from Temple services. However, God tells them that if they observe the Sabbath, practice justice and righteousness with their neighbor, and keep his covenant, they will be accepted by God in the presence of his people and be able to minister service (v. 6) to the LORD at the Temple. This backdrop helps to shed even greater light on the actions and words of Jesus. Although the immediate application of Isaiah 56 might have been intended for the returning captives, the spirit of this passage should have continued throughout their generations. The Jews of Jesus' day failed to keep the spirit of God's grace toward the outcasts. They denied them their honored place of worship before God and, therefore, withheld his blessing for them as guests in his house.

Second, by quoting the Isaiah passage in the first person when referring to the Temple as *my house,* Jesus claims the words in Isaiah as his own. Therefore, he speaks as the one who initially issued this assurance. In John 2:16, he called the Temple "My Father's house." No one had ever before referred to the Temple as *my* Father's House. For a man to refer to God as his Father in such a personal way was considered blasphemous. By doing so, Jesus was not simply claiming equality with the Father. He was claiming his Father's possessions as his own. Therefore, by dishonoring the foreigner in his house, they expressed dishonor toward the Master of the house. This completes his second Messianic act of the week.

ACT THREE

Jesus' third Messianic act was the restoring of sight to the blind and the healing of the lame at the Temple, prompting the children to shout, "Hosanna to the Son of David" (Matt. 21:14–15). As already mentioned in chapter six, *Kingdom Parables in Jewish Soil,* three miracles were considered reserved for the Messiah: healing of the leper, giving sight to the blind (Isa. 61:1–2), and the healing of the deaf and mute. These signs convinced some of the priests. John records that by this time, some Jewish leaders believed in him but remained silent about their faith, fearing the ruling Pharisees and Sanhedrin. These were the same ones who demanded that Jesus silence the children (John 12:42). In sharp reply to their demands, Jesus quoted Psalm 8:2 from the Septuagint, the Greek version of the Hebrew Bible: "From the lips of children and infants, you have ordained praise." Again, in typical ancient rabbinic style, by quoting only a part of the passage, he implicated his opponents with what was left unquoted. The portion left for his adversaries to recall (and they did) reads, "because of thine enemies; that thou mightest put down the enemy and avenger" (Psalm 8:2b, Brenton LXX). The indictment was clear. They had positioned themselves as enemies of God. This, of course, insulted them, so they sought a way to kill him. This ended the events of the second day of the Passion Week and the third Messianic act. Jesus left them and went back to Bethany for the night.

Food for Thought

1. The picture of a royal wedding was a common image in Jewish teaching. What did this image communicate to the devout Jew?

2. What week in the life of Christ does this parable highlight?

3. What was the first of four Messianic acts of Jesus during this week?

4. Discuss the significance of the phrase *Son of David* in Jewish thought.

5. What was Jesus' second Messianic act? Discuss its relationship to the Gentiles.

6. Discuss the implication of Jesus' words when he referred to the Temple as "My Father's house." Why was this viewed as a blasphemous statement by the Jews?

7. What was Jesus' third Messianic act? Discuss the children's response and how it relates to what was expected of the Messiah at his revelation.

8. What is the most meaningful thing you learned from this lesson?

Chapter 19

The Parable of the Royal Wedding Banquet, Part Two

ACT FOUR
Leading Up to the Parable of the Royal Wedding Banquet

On the third day, Jesus arrived again in Jerusalem, teaching in the Temple courts and preaching the Good News of the Kingdom (Matt. 21:23; Mark 11:27; Luke 20:1). Teaching and proclaiming the Good News of the Kingdom was his fourth Messianic act at the Temple, as the prophet Isaiah had foretold of the Messiah (52:7; 61:1). Here, we hear him speak a series of three parables ending with the Parable of the Royal Wedding Banquet. First, we need to examine what led up to these parables. A debate can be expected. The Jewish leaders interrupted him with their interrogation by challenging his Messianic authority. "By what authority are you doing these things?" they demanded (Matt. 21:23; Mark 11:28; Luke 20:2). By *authority*, we assume they are referring to governmental authority from their misguided view of things. However, bear in mind the third Messianic act from the previous day. The miracles Jesus performed the day before should have settled any questions about the source of his authority. Only God can restore sight to the blind, another Messianic sign they denied. God's signature was evident enough for the common people to respond with Messianic praise. The dispute with him indicates their question was intended as a trap. To avoid their entrapment, Jesus questioned them about the authority of the baptism of John, whether it was of God or men. They refused to answer on grounds of self-incrimination and for fear of the people. Therefore, Jesus refused to answer their question.

Knowing that Jesus never asks an arbitrary question, why did he choose a question about the authority of John's baptism? What does this have to do with the question raised by his antagonists and the three parables that will follow? Is there a connection? There is! The baptism of John and the acts of Jesus share the exact source of authority. John's baptism was not intended to be another ceremonial immersion in water added to the ones the Jews were already practicing. This immersion was by faith in the coming Messiah and was associated with the presence and promises of God's reign (kingdom). Through John and Jesus, God was calling Israel to repentance because the reign of heaven was at hand. The time of the Messiah was being fulfilled. That is, John and Jesus proclaimed that God's reign was already being demonstrated in their presence.

The Gospels of Mark and Luke also tell us that John was preaching "a baptism of repentance for forgiveness of sins" (Mark 1:4; Luke 3:3). Forgiveness of sins was not a new concept to Israel. The Torah taught that justification has always been by faith—Abraham as their example. However, the pronouncement of forgiveness of sins in the way John and Jesus did it was an act believed to be held in reserve for the Messiah as "an act of total liberation," says Arias (21). It was announcing the Year of Jubilee by announcing the Messiah's reign. Arias further writes, "To announce the Kingdom is to restore life, to promise life, to celebrate life" (22). *Restore, promise,* and *celebrate* are key words in his statement. I want to add one thing here. This was the first time the forgiveness of sins was not connected to the sacrificial system. This was huge.

Therefore, when the Pharisees refused to be baptized by John (Luke 7:30) and rejected Jesus, they cast aside their part in the promises of the reign of Messiah, the forgiveness of sins, and consequently, eternal life. They rejected the restoration of the Kingdom to Israel and the celebration around the table of the Abraham. This sets the stage for three parables. Here are the first two parables with their applications.

Parable One: The Parable of the Two Sons (recorded only by Matthew)

Matthew 21:28–32

What do you think? There was a man who had two sons. He went to the first and said, "Son, go and work today in the vineyard." "I will not," he answered, but later he changed his mind and went. Then the father went to the other son and said the same thing. He answered, "I will, sir," but he did not go. "Which of the two did what his father wanted?" "The first," they answered. Jesus said to them, "I tell you the truth, the tax collectors and the prostitutes are entering the Kingdom of God ahead of you. For John came to you to show you the way of righteousness, and you did not believe him, but the tax collectors and the prostitutes did. And even after you saw this, you did not repent and believe him."

Application: Jesus said, "I tell you the truth, the tax collectors and prostitutes are entering the Kingdom of God ahead of you."

Parable Two: The Parable of the Vineyard and the Wicked Tenants

Matthew 21:33–43; Mark 12:1–9; Luke 20:9–16

He then began to speak to them in parables: "A man planted a vineyard. He put a wall around it, dug a pit for the winepress and built a watchtower. Then he rented the vineyard to some farmers and went away on a journey. At harvest time he sent a servant to the tenants to collect from them some of the fruit of the vineyard. But they seized him, beat him and sent him away empty-handed. Then he sent another servant to them;

they struck this man on the head and treated him shamefully. He sent still another, and that one they killed. He sent many others; some of them they beat, others they killed. He had one left to send, a son, whom he loved. He sent him last of all, saying, "They will respect my son." But the tenants said to one another, "This is the heir. Come, let us kill him, and the inheritance will be ours." So they took him and killed him, and threw him out of the vineyard." What then will the owner of the vineyard do? He will come and kill those tenants and give the vineyard to others.

Application: Jesus said, "Therefore I tell you that the Kingdom of God will be taken away from you and given to a people who will produce its fruit."

When we combine the applications of both parables, we have this message to the Sanhedrin and the Jewish elite. *The Reign of God will be taken away from you and given to those you have cast out. They are entering the Reign of God instead of you and will produce its fruit.*

This must have been like fingernails on a chalkboard to the ears of the Pharisees. Tax collectors and prostitutes were two extremes on both ends of a class of people the Pharisees despised. They called them the *am ha-aretz* or the People of the Land. It was a derogatory term. These comprised the masses. One rabbi said that because of the *am ha-aretz,* God punishes the world (Fosdick 123). They were considered by the piously religious as outcasts and non-covenanted people. They were mostly uneducated, thought to be immoral, non-practicing Jews who had no respect for Pharisaic Judaism. You might say they were the *unchurched* of their day. Neither of the two most prominent schools of the Pharisees (Shammai or Hillel) had anything good to say about this sub-class of people, even though the Pharisees of the school of Hillel were more evangelistic toward them. Still, the overall discrimination and outright disdain toward them were well known. What a shock and an insult it must have been to hear Jesus turn the tables on the Pharisees, making *them* the outcasts. Then again, how welcome that must have been for those who were victims of Pharisaic prejudice and self-righteous arrogance.

The Vineyard

Before we read of Jesus adding fuel to the fire, we must point out something significant that could go unnoticed. Both of the parables we have just read speak of a vineyard. Drawing from Jewish backgrounds, this is connected with the Vineyard Song of Isaiah 5:1–7. In the Septuagint, this passage reads:

> Now I will sing to my beloved a song of my beloved concerning his vineyard. My beloved had a vineyard on a high hill in a fertile place. And I made a hedge round it, and dug a trench, and planted a choice vine, and built a tower in the midst of it and dug a place for the wine-vat in it: and I waited for it to bring forth grapes, and it brought forth thorns. And now, ye dwellers in Jerusalem, and every man of Judah, judge between me and my vineyard. What shall I do any more to my vineyard, that I have not done to it? Whereas I expected it to bring forth grapes, but it has brought forth thorns. And now I will tell you what I will do to my vineyard: I will take away its hedge, and it shall be for a spoil; and I will pull down its walls, and it shall be left to be trodden down. And I will forsake my vineyard; and it shall not be pruned, nor dug, and thorns shall come upon it as on barren land; and I will command the clouds to rain no rain upon it. For the vineyard of the Lord of hosts is the house of Israel, and the men of Judah his beloved plant. I expected it to bring forth judgment, and it brought forth iniquity; and not righteousness, but a cry (Isa. 5:1–7, Brenton LXX).

The reason for choosing because it appears to be the one Matthew and Mark alluded to as they quoted Jesus. Notice the parallels of the beginning verses:

Isaiah	Mark
My beloved had a vineyard	A man planted a vineyard
I made a hedge around it	I put a wall around it

Isaiah	Mark
And dug a trench	Dug a pit for a winepress
Planted a choice vine	(no parallel)
Built a tower in the midst of it	Built a watchtower

The similarities end here, but this was enough to drive the application home. From this point onward, Jesus changes the content of Isaiah's song to add insult to injury with a customized storyline. Once more, we find Jesus using scripture as a Jewish rabbi would be expected. He makes an abbreviated allusion to a certain passage, leaving the inference for his listeners to connect. But what was he inferring by this? Jeremias points out, "It is at once apparent from the allusions to the scripture in the first sentences that the reference is not to an earthly owner of a vineyard and to his vineyard, but to God and Israel" (Jeremias 70). A vineyard was a metaphor, having roots deep within the prophets. God often spoke of Israel as his vineyard (cf. Psalm 80:9). Jesus was accusing the leaders of Jerusalem of being guilty of the same sins as those of Isaiah's day. They had failed to bear the fruit of justice and righteousness. Because of this, Jerusalem—the vineyard on the hill— will be destroyed, leaving the Kingdom of God to be given to others who will produce the fruit he desires.

The implication of these two parables is therefore obvious. Jesus presents himself not only as a prophet but as the Messiah with the authority to render judgment upon Jerusalem, incriminating the corrupt Jewish elite. Luke records the shock in the people's reaction to the Parable of the Vineyard and the Wicked Tenants as saying, "May it never be!" (Luke 20:16) They clearly understood the vineyard as representing Jerusalem and the Temple and the meaning behind his parables.

Food for Thought

1. Why did Jesus choose a question about the authority of John's baptism?

2. What is the application of the Parable of the Two Sons? Discuss how this would have insulted the Jewish leadership.

3. What is the application of the Parable of the Vineyard and the Wicked Tenants? What did it have to say to the Jewish leadership?

4. What was Jesus inferring by his use of the Septuagint version of the Parable of the Vineyard in Isaiah chapter five?

5. Summarize these applications intended for the Jewish leaders.

6. What is the most meaningful thing you learned from this lesson?

Chapter 20

The Murdered Son and a Rejected Stone

Connecting the Parable of the Vineyard and the Wicked Tenants with the Parable of the Royal Wedding Banquet is a Hebrew parable taken from Psalm 118:22. Again, those standing within hearing distance of Jesus expressed shock at his implications. In response to the people's dismay and disbelief, Jesus looked at them and said, "What then is this that is written: 'The very stone which the builders rejected has become the head of the corner'?" Jesus adds, "Every one who falls on that stone will be broken to pieces; but when it falls on any one it will crush him" (Luke 20:17–18 RSV).

Those who have looked at this from the Hebrew and Aramaic languages see a play on words between the word *son* in the Parable of the Vineyard and the Wicked Tenants and the word *stone* in the Psalm quotation. First, the son in the Parable of the Vineyard and the Wicked Tenants is an *only* son. This is seen even in the Greek and translated as *beloved son*. Both the Greek word and its Hebrew equivalent are in agreement. This is the same word expressed by the Father in heaven toward Jesus at his baptism (Matt. 3:17). The word *stone* refers to David, according to Jewish tradition. The stone the builders rejected was interpreted as King David, describing how Samuel and Jesse overlooked him in choosing the second king of Israel (Young 313). Second, the word *son* in Hebrew is *ben*. The Hebrew word for *stone* is *eben*. It appears that Jesus was taking the Jewish interpretation of Psalm 118:22, attaching the implication of David to the beloved son in the vineyard parable and turning it into a reference to the Son of David. This certainly fits the context. This would, therefore, make the son killed in the vineyard symbolize the murder of the Messiah, the Son of David, by the Jewish leaders.

Application

Jesus did not give an interpretation to the Parable of the Royal Wedding Banquet, as he did with the previous two. However, it was common for a Jewish rabbi to expect his listeners to apply the appropriate application. This parable comes at the climax of three days of controversy between Jesus and the religious leaders in Jerusalem. The events, the actions, and the words of the last few days had been brought together to this one moment and summarized into one parable. The Parable of the Royal Wedding Banquet implicated the Jewish elite as having sinned against the king. As in the parable before this one, they are the ones who have the blood of the vineyard owner's only son on their hands and the ones who rejected the invitation seized his servants and killed them. Therefore, as a prophetic judgment and warning to the Jewish leaders of Jerusalem, the parable describes an angry king who destroys his enemies and burns their city, removing them from his dominion. Once the king removes them, he invites outcasts, tax collectors, and prostitutes, as well as new guests who are both "good and bad," to fill his wedding hall.

His indictment could not be clearer. By connecting the vineyard metaphor, they identified the burned city as Jerusalem –specifically the Temple. They likewise understood the meaning and significance of the banquet very well. During this Intertestamental period, there was an increase in apocalyptic writing with emphasis on the Messianic banquet. The banquet symbolized salvation and deliverance. It was unthinkable in the minds of the Jewish elite that they would be rejected and replaced by the despicable *am ha-aretz* whom they did not deem worthy of salvation. This was the ultimate insult, a slap to their self-righteous faces.

The Wedding Garment

Many scholars believe that the Parable of the Royal Wedding Banquet combines two parables. The second part of the parable describes one guest without a wedding garment, who is noticed by the king and cast out when he cannot explain himself. As there were

Messianic implications associated with the banquet, in Jewish thought, there were Messianic implications associated with the wedding garments of the guests. They both symbolized salvation. Salvation was also associated with the bride's wedding gown. Regarding Israel's salvation from bondage, Paul describes the nation as having been "baptized into Moses in the cloud and in the sea" (1 Cor. 10:2). The prophet Ezekiel describes the nation's emergence from that *baptism* into her beautiful womanhood. God "adorned [her] with gold and silver; … fine linen and costly fabric and embroidered cloth" (Ezek. 16:13). Israel was clothed in the beautiful gown of salvation. She became his queen. But as we continue to read, she soon begins to trust in her beauty and becomes adulterous. This was the indictment Jesus was vigorously raising. The Jewish leaders were making the same mistakes their ancestors had made, but this time, their crimes were in the presence of their Messiah. Consequently, their judgment will be more severe.

Picturing God as a Gracious Jewish Host

Jewish literature of the late Second Temple period is filled with references to this connection of banqueting with the Messiah. It, too, is a picture of salvation at its most fundamental level. In Isaiah 25:6, between hymns of thanksgiving and rejoicing is a picture of the Messianic banquet:

On this mountain the LORD Almighty will prepare a feast of rich food for all peoples, a banquet of aged wine—the best of meats and the finest of wines.

Although this theme has varying beliefs and usages, banquets prepared by God in the Hebrew Scriptures supplied ancient Jewish literature with rich imagery.[16] The Book of Exodus records Israel being invited to God's table. It is interesting that after the Exodus, whenever the presence of God is connected with banqueting, God is always represented as the Host and Master of Ceremonies. Shortly after they arrived at Mount Sinai, the nation of Israel began its covenant relationship with God by being invited to a banquet on the holy mountain. Exodus 24 records a meeting between God and representatives of Israel. There was Moses, Aaron and his sons, and seventy of the elders of Israel. Verses 10–11 record, "and [they] saw the God of Israel. Under his feet was something like a pavement made of sapphire, clear as the sky itself. But God did not raise his hand against these leaders of the Israelites; they saw God, and they ate and drank." This is amazing! God prepared a banquet before the shepherds and leaders of Israel.

Another example is found in the peace offering (or fellowship offering). It was a festive Levitical sacrifice recognizing God as the Host. The final stage of the ritual of the offering commanded that the remainder of the meat of the animal (what was not burned on the altar) was to be enjoyed in a feast inviting the officiating priest, the worshiper, his family, the Levite within his gates; widows; orphans; and his household servants. It was designed to be a community affair celebrating reconciliation, thanksgiving, and friendship with God. This banquet was also to be celebrated within the courtyard of the Tabernacle, or Temple, to honor and recognize God as the Host of the banquet. Moses said, "There, in the presence of the Lord your God, you and your families shall eat and shall rejoice" (Deut. 12:7, 17–18; 16:11). David also wrote about a table prepared by the LORD in the presence of his enemies (Psalm 23:5). We do not often picture God as a gracious host, but this is how he chooses to reveal himself (Arias 29). The God of Israel loves celebrating with his people, inviting all willing to come. He does not take the refusal of his invitation lightly.

Conclusion

The Reign of God, as described in the Parable of the Royal Wedding Banquet, demonstrates the tragedy of unbelief. When the Son of David is rejected, the Father is rejected with him. However, their refusal to honor his right to rule does not rule out his right to judgment and his authority to banish those who dishonor the King from the Messianic banquet. His Kingdom rules over all, whether they honor his sovereignty or not. This parable, along with the other parables associated with it, illustrates how the Jewish leaders rejected the King's invitation and lost their seats at the Messianic banquet, leaving an opportunity for those who accepted it.

However, the power of this message shows us that it is not enough to respond to the invitation simply. We must be clothed with the wedding garment. We, who have been immersed in water, with faith in the Son of David, are clothed with him, the Apostle says in Galatians 3:27. The wedding garment serves as a significant image in this picture because of the salvation it represents and the status it provides in relation to the King's Son.

This parable will be combined with two more Kingdom Parables to solidify the decree announcing judgment upon Jerusalem. But there will also be a message of hope for the remnant and the promise of vindication for the righteous.

Food for Thought

1. Discuss how God is viewed as a gracious Host from the Old Testament.

2. According to Jewish tradition, who represented the stone the builders rejected?

3. Who is the stone the builders rejected, and who are the builders, according to Jesus?

4. How is God pictured throughout Israel's history concerning banqueting?

5. What does the wedding garment symbolize?

6. What is the most meaningful thing you learned from this lesson?

Chapter 21

The Parable of the Ten Maidens

Matthew 25:1–13

The last two parables in our study are the Parables of the Ten Maidens and the Talents. The first of these remaining two Kingdom Parables is set again against a first-century Jewish wedding. Just as Peter warned before his death around A.D. 67 not to become impatient about the Lord's coming (cf. 2 Pet. 3:8, 14), this parable is about preparation, patience, and preventative measures. Though these parables are not the most complex, their contexts bear a complexity we must consider. Both deal with the *comings* of the Lord. On one side of the parables, we have a context prophesying the coming of Christ in judgment against Jerusalem, bringing the end of the Jewish age. On the other side, we have the prophecy of the coming of Christ in judgment on all the nations at the end of time. In conclusion, I will present an application of these two events as both parables share them. Here is the Parable of the Ten Maidens:

> At that time, the Kingdom of heaven will be like ten Maidens who took their lamps and went out to meet the bridegroom. Five of them were foolish and five were wise. The foolish ones took their lamps but did not take any oil with them. The wise, however, took oil in jars along with their lamps. The bridegroom was a long time in coming, and they all became drowsy and fell asleep. At midnight the cry rang out: "Here's the bridegroom! Come out to meet him!" Then all the Maidens woke up and trimmed their lamps. The foolish ones said to the wise, "Give us some of your oil; our lamps are going out." "No," they replied, 'there may not be enough for both us and you.

Instead, go to those who sell oil and buy some for yourselves." But while they were on their way to buy the oil, the bridegroom arrived. The Maidens who were ready went in with him to the wedding banquet. And the door was shut. Later the others also came. "Sir! Sir!" they said. "Open the door for us!" But he replied, "I tell you the truth, I don't know you." Therefore keep watch, because you do not know the day or the hour.

Jewish Background

The Parable of the Ten Maidens again reflects the customs of a first-century Jewish wedding. Unlike the Parable of the Royal Wedding Banquet, this parable does not focus on the celebration, the banquet, the guests, or the father of the groom. Instead, Jesus directs our attention to ten girls who hurried to participate in a wedding procession. The wedding of a young Jewish couple typically took place on the third day of the week to allow ample time after the weekly Sabbath for preparation. After a full day of celebration with guests at the home of the bride's parents, nightfall brought the expectation of the next stage of the festivities. Sometime after darkness settled in, the groom was expected to leave his parent's house with a small company of friends. The custom was to deliberately delay his arrival as he bargained for the gifts he prepared to give to his future in-laws. To arrive too early might express a lack of respect for her family. It was customary to express respect for her parents' reluctance to give their daughter away. By waiting until the last minute, she was able to remain in her parents' home a little longer before the ceremony. As the groom approached the bride's house, messengers announced his arrival. Joined by a lamp-lit procession of joyous celebrators, music, and giggling girls, the couple was formally escorted back to the groom's home, where the celebration resumed. Once everyone was inside, the door was closed, and the ceremony began. Anyone not part of the wedding procession could not enter once the door was closed.

An Image of God and Israel

The parable introduces ten girls with lamps burning that were typically tied to the tops of poles, awaiting the coming of the groom to fetch his bride. This use of lamps or candles had a historical likeness connecting the Jewish wedding to the beginning of Israel's relationship as God's bride. According to the rabbis, the lights of these lamps were intended to recall Exodus 20:18: "When the people saw the thunder and lightning and heard the trumpet and saw the mountain in smoke, they trembled with fear." God is seen as coming to Israel accompanied by flashing light. Another interesting likeness pictures Moses as the friend of the bridegroom. "Then Moses led the people out of the camp to meet with God, and they stood at the foot of the mountain" (Exo. 19:17). The rabbis linked these events to the groom arriving by the light of lamps and the friend of the groom escorting the bride to join her betrothed husband. It was yet another way for the Jews to rehearse and celebrate the story of their deliverance from Egypt.

The contrast between the wise and the *foolish* is also a familiar Jewish theme. Solomon is, of course, considered the wisest man in ancient Jewish history to make use of this extensively in his Proverbs and the Book of Ecclesiastes. For example, "Better a poor but wise youth than an old but foolish king who no longer knows how to take warning" (Ecc. 4:13). Wisdom literature in Jewish writings heightened during the late Second Temple period. Its influence on Jewish thought should be considered an important part of the backdrop of these culturally conditioned texts. Therefore, when Jesus contrasted the five wise girls with the five foolish girls, he reflected themes that were commonly heard in Jewish wisdom and rabbinic teaching with a backdrop that rehearses the history of Israel.

The Context

In the opening of this chapter, it was mentioned that the context bears a certain complexity. The parable is part of a more extensive discussion between Jesus and the disciples on the Mount of Olives while admiring the panoramic view of Jerusalem and the Temple (Matt. 24:3; Mark 13:3). As they boasted about the magnificent architecture of the Temple, Jesus said, "I tell you the truth, not one stone will be left on another; everyone will be thrown down" (Matt. 24:2). The question within a broader context is whether or not Jesus was speaking only of the A.D. 70 destruction of Jerusalem, or was he speaking of both the destruction of the Temple *and* of his second coming at the end of time? For the most part, you will find the latter being taken up.

The Parable of the Ten Maidens interpretation hinges on a demonstrative adverb of time that connects it to the Matthew 24 event. The New International Version renders Matthew 25:1 as "At that time the Kingdom of heaven will be like …" The question we need to consider is this—what *time* is it being announced? To answer that question, we must consider Matthew 24:3, Mark 13:4, and Luke 21:7, where the disciples are asked three questions:
1. When will Jerusalem be destroyed?
2. What will be the sign of the destruction?
3. What will be the sign of your [Jesus] coming and of the end of the age?

To answer the first and second questions, Jesus said, "When you see Jerusalem being surrounded by armies, you will know that its desolation is near" (Luke 21:20). This was about the Roman invasion by Generals Vespasian and Titus. Josephus, a negotiator for these generals with the Jewish authorities, has left us the most thoroughly documented account of the Jewish wars, most notably the second destruction of Jerusalem in A.D. 70. In his lengthy eyewitness account, he describes a prolonged and blood-soaked conflict both within and outside of the city. It could have been averted had the rebels (led by just a few renegades) surrendered before it escalated out of control. Believing that God was behind their rebellion, they remained defiant to the very end. They killed many of those who tried to surrender, though some did manage to escape with their lives. Toward the end, however, General Titus began ordering the evacuees to be crucified. Not until the Holocaust of WWII was there such a wholesale slaughter of the Jewish people.

From Matthew 24, Mark 13, Luke 17 and 21, we are told three things that need addressing because of the nature of the language. First, the sign of the coming Son of Man was visible (Matt. 24:30; Mark 13:26; Luke 21:27). Many misread and misinterpreted this section because of the apocalyptic speech and our tendency to literalize prophetic images. A brief review of the Old Testament prophets will help us see that Jesus uses the familiar language of judgment borrowed from the prophets to describe his judgment upon Jerusalem (Isa. 13:1, 9–10; 19:1; 34:4; Ezek. 32:1–8; Joel 2:24–32; Psalm 18:7–12.). As R.T. France writes, "The destruction of the capital and the temple of the nation which had hitherto been the focus of divine government on earth marked a change in the divine economy so profound as to justify the vivid apocalyptic symbolism of cosmic collapse, which the Old Testament prophets had used of the downfall of Babylon and other pagan powers" (79). With this type of imagery, the Old Testament prophets describe many *comings* of God executing His judgment upon the nations of the earth.

The passage most recalled here is Daniel 7:13, which reads, "In my vision at night I looked, and there before me was one like a son of man, coming with the clouds of heaven. He approached the Ancient of Days and was led into his presence." This is a vision that the Jewish rabbis understood as the enthronement of the Messiah. By saying, "At that time men will see the Son of Man coming in clouds with great power and glory" (Mark 13:26), Jesus established for the disciples and subsequent generations that the A.D. 70 destruction was his act of judgment executed as the enthroned Messiah.

Second, the destruction of Jerusalem marked the end of the Jewish era, and its destruction became a witness to the presence of the Kingdom of Heaven. Remember that the Jews associated the phrase *Kingdom of Heaven* with God's active rule being demonstrated on the earth. Therefore, the Roman invasion was interpreted by the early Jewish Christians as the visible sign of the presence (*parousia*) of the enthroned Messiah coming in judgment upon Jerusalem.

Finally, the time-frame for "all these things" was within that generation (Luke 21:31). This critical detail (often overlooked) is a vital consideration regarding the third question asked by the disciples. It depends upon how we interpret the *end of the age*. Matthew is the only one who records the disciples asking about its sign. If you will recall once again, from our study of the *Parable of the Weeds in the Field* in chapters nine and ten, and our study of the *Parable of the Dragnet* in Chapter Thirteen, we dealt with the phrase *end of the age* as referring to the end of the Jewish era just as Daniel had predicted it (Dan. 9:27). It was noted that many want to interpret this as referring to the end of the world rather than the end of the Jewish era. But this interpretation propels the application of this prophecy to some future time well beyond that generation. Matthew, Mark, and Luke record Jesus as saying, "Even so, **when you see these things happening**, you know that the Kingdom of God is nearby. I tell you the truth, **this generation will certainly not pass away until all these things have happened**" (emphasis mine). Therefore, we must conclude that Jesus spoke entirely about the end of the Jewish age. It was the end of that era in history for the Jewish nation. You cannot talk of a first-century generation on one hand and interpret it as a generation at the end of time.

The Jewish Nation—A Closed Door

I think it is difficult for us in our 21st century Western culture to empathize with the Jews of the first century. Jerusalem and the Temple were the center of their universe. To hear these words of judgment and destruction coming directly from the Messiah must have been as upsetting as when God foretold of Jerusalem's first destruction to the prophet Habakkuk. The reaction was one of disbelief.

There is an old Jewish proverb that says, "A door that has been closed is not quickly opened." This seems to be the sentiment of the Parable of the Ten Maidens. Once the door was closed, we read of the five foolish girls returning late and pleading for the door to be opened for them. "'Sir! Sir!' they said. 'Open the door for us!' But he replied, 'I tell you the truth, I do not know you.'" Just as Jesus reveals himself in the Book of Revelation as the one who holds the "key of David," who opens what no one can shut and shuts what no one can open, he presents himself as the one who possesses the authority to grant or forbid entrance into his fellowship. As for those on the outside, he announces, "I will have nothing to do with you" (Jeremias 175). History records that tens of thousands remembered the warning when the Romans surrounded Jerusalem, but many did not. For them, the door to the Kingdom of the Messiah had closed.

Application

I realize that my analysis, or lack thereof, is too brief. Space will not allow me to present a more thorough treatment of Matthew 24 with Mark and Luke, respectively, because it would divert our attention away from our aim. I hope to have established the following proposition within practical limitations. *The Parable of the Ten Maidens was intended for those who would experience the end of the Jewish era.* It was "at that time" some were found watching and others were not, as the presence of the Son of Man demonstrated his reign through the destructive Roman war machine, causing the powers of heaven to be shaken for the Jewish people (cf. Luke 21:20–27). With this in mind, the parable has a time-frame, and the details of the parable are given a greater definition without having to allegorize their meaning.

To interpret the bridegroom as representing Jesus, I think, is correct even though the Old Testament and Jewish literature of the late Second Temple period do not portray the Messiah as a bridegroom. This, then, would be a new image of the Messiah presented by Jesus and one that claims deity. Yes, there is a discussion between Jesus and a group of Pharisees about the issue of fasting, where he compares himself to a bridegroom. Still, there is no obvious Messianic association in that passage. John the Baptizer comes closer by comparing himself to the bridegroom's friend. John said, "The bride belongs to the bridegroom. The friend who attends the bridegroom waits and listens for him and is joyful when he hears the bridegroom's voice. That joy is mine, and it is now complete" (John 3:29). This context is Messianic.

Conclusion

Jesus presents himself as the bridegroom in the parable, which is yet another example of assigning to himself what was formerly identified with the God of Israel. The apostles Paul and John also use this new likeness in their writings to the churches (cf. 2 Cor. 11:2; Eph. 5:23–32; Rev. 19:7–9; 21:1–2). It was an image of Christ and the church that the early Christians readily accepted because of the Old Testament parallel between God and the nation of Israel.

As stated in the opening of this chapter, the Parable of the Ten Maidens presents a sense of urgency for preparation and patience while admonishing watchfulness. The immediate application is intended for the first-century generation. Jesus makes this clear. However, we of the 21st century should take to heart that the return of Jesus is equally imminent. Whether speaking of the *comings* of God's judgment throughout human history or at the end of history with the final Coming of Christ, his judgment shares many of the same characteristics. Jesus *is* coming in judgment. Therefore, we must be prepared. The need to be vigilant for the bridegroom's appearance must be our aim. Otherwise, we, too, will be found outside of his favor and, therefore, in that realm of his Kingdom where he rules with a rod of iron.

Food for Thought

1. Discuss the details of a traditional first-century wedding and the relationship of these details to the Exodus and Moses.

2. What topic discussed by Jesus and the disciples set the stage for the Parable of the Ten Maidens?

3. What three questions were asked by the disciples?

4. Discuss R.T. Frances' statement as it relates to the context.

5. How did Jewish-Christians interpret the Roman invasion of Judea in the first century?

6. What is the time frame Jesus gave for the event that corresponds with this parable prophesied in Matthew 24, Mark 13, and Luke 21?

7. Discuss the immediate application for the Parable of the Ten Maidens.

8. What new image of the Messiah is introduced in this parable that is associated with God in the Old Testament?

9. What is the most meaningful thing you learned from this lesson?

Chapter 22

The Parable of the Talents

Matthew 25:14–30

Our last parable to consider in our study of the Kingdom Parables of Christ is one about an aristocrat who entrusted his wealth to three of his most trusted servants, intending for them to make investments. This parable continues the discourse between Jesus and his disciples on the Mount of Olives. It immediately follows the Parable of the Ten Maidens. The mood is somber. Two days are left before Jesus' last Passover and his crucifixion—the last Passover to fulfill all Passovers. Jesus reveals things to the disciples that they cannot fully comprehend, much less imagine—heartrending things.

He tells them that Jerusalem and the Temple will be destroyed. Not one stone will be left on another. But it was not the destruction of the Temple that was grieving him. His grief was directed toward a people who did not recognize the time of God's coming and for the needless catastrophe because they had not turned their hearts toward God. They had rejected the Messiah, but that was not entirely the cause of their judgment. The scales had already been tipped against them for killing the prophets and stoning those who were sent to them (Matt. 23:37). Add to this the weight of the next few days, knowing he would be handed over by one of his own to be crucified. It was time to leave the ones he trusted the most while entrusting them with his Messianic assignment. So, with this as the setting, Jesus spoke another parable to them, emphasizing what he had already taught them: responsibility, patience, and warning—but now, he will add accountability. Here is the Parable of the Talents:

Again, it will be like a man going on a journey who called his servants and entrusted his property to them. To one he gave five talents of money, to another two talents, and to another one talent, each according to his ability. Then he went on his journey. The man who had received the five talents went at once and put his money to work and gained five more. So also, the one with the two talents gained two more. But the man who had received the one talent went off, dug a hole in the ground and hid his master's money. After a long time the master of those servants returned and settled accounts with them. The man who had received the five talents brought the other five. "Master," he said, "you entrusted me with five talents. See, I have gained five more." His master replied, "Well done, good and faithful servant! You have been faithful with a few things; I will put you in charge of many things. Come and share your master's happiness!" The man with the two talents also came. "Master," he said, "you entrusted me with two talents; see, I have gained two more." His master replied, "Well done, good and faithful servant! You have been faithful with a few things; I will put you in charge of many things. Come and share your master's happiness!" Then the man who had received the one talent came. "Master," he said, "I knew that you are a hard man, harvesting where you have not sown and gathering where you have not scattered seed. So I was afraid and went out and hid your talent in the ground. See, here is what belongs to you." His master replied, "You wicked, lazy servant! So you knew that I harvest where I have not sown and gather where I have not scattered seed? Well then, you should have put my money on deposit with the bankers so that when I returned, I would have received it back with interest. "Take the talent from him and give it to the one who has the ten talents. For everyone who has will be given more, and he will have an abundance. Whoever does not have, even what he has will be taken from him. And throw that worthless servant outside, into the darkness, where there will be weeping and gnashing of teeth."

Jewish or Gentile Background

The background of this parable could be Jewish or Gentile. The master is a wealthy landlord, an aristocrat, and a member of the upper two percent of the population, whose wealth places him among the controlling elite. His business requires him to leave his enterprise at home and leave it to trusted servants to manage while he is away. He is wealthy enough to travel to other countries. This was something few, in that day and time, could do. This ruler could have been involved in many profitable endeavors, but judging from his description, he appears to be an unscrupulous land-grabber. As in most cases, the ambition of a covetous ruler was to acquire as much land as possible since owning land increased his authority.

As in our study of the Parable of the Merciful King, large sums of money play a part in this parable in the form of talents. If the Master's goods were in the form of silver, a talent of silver was roughly worth six thousand denarii. If a day laborer worked for one denarius per day –an average wage, it would take nearly twenty years to earn one talent of silver. The first slave was entrusted with five talents. The second slave was entrusted with two talents. The third was entrusted with one. Even this lesser amount represents the master's extreme trust in the loyalty of his servants. They were expected to invest their Master's goods, assuming it was money, or at the very least, deposit it to earn interest. Doing nothing with what they had been given was not an option.

In Jewish thought, this parable would have resembled rabbinic teachings on investing yourself personally in studying the Torah. From chapter two, *Approaching the Sacred Text*, it was commonly taught that paradise was assured if a person could comprehend the depths of wisdom and knowledge of just one passage. Failure or neglect to invest oneself in the study and meditation of the Torah and the *Mishnah* was considered an abuse of the Torah. The Jews viewed the Torah as having been entrusted to them by God and, therefore, a precious gift. Paul even writes of this Jewish advantage over the Gentiles in Romans 3:2, saying that "they [the Jews] have been entrusted with the very words of God." He uses the word "entrusted" in the same way the servants in this parable were entrusted with their Master's wealth and were expected to use it wisely. Though they failed to be faithful stewards of this divine trust, they considered the Torah a sacred trust to be returned to God with interest.

The Context

In the previous parable, the Parable of the Ten Maidens, the context follows Jesus' prediction of the destruction of Jerusalem. The parable is linked to this event. The Parable of the Talents is directly connected to this discussion. It, too, is a Kingdom Parable, though it does not begin with a likeness to the Kingdom. Some English versions, unfortunately, add the words "For the Kingdom of heaven is like…" to verse fourteen, which causes a break in the continuity of thought from verse thirteen. It is within this admonition that we find the purpose of this parable.

Immediate Application

It is difficult to picture the disciples being stoically indifferent as Jesus revealed these things. Disbelief and shock must have overwhelmed them as Jesus revealed the end of the age and the extent of the destruction of Jerusalem. This closely resembles the days recorded by the prophets, particularly Jeremiah, Daniel, and Ezekiel. As with the disciples, there was a sense of disbelief from the nation of Judah as they were told how Jerusalem was about to be destroyed by Babylon. While Jeremiah predicted devastation and urged Judah to surrender, false prophets were preaching their messages of peace and safety and sought to discredit Jeremiah as a traitor. Meanwhile, in Babylonian exile, Ezekiel was considered a lunatic for predicting the same, and Daniel was portrayed as a rebel against the king.

To comfort the remnant of Israel in Babylonian captivity, Ezekiel Chapters 34 - 48 describe a coming glory in language filled with idioms and figures of speech that the Jews could readily identify and understand. They needed to know that the Torah, God's righteousness, which they upheld, and the promises of God would be vindicated and fulfilled. Speaking through Ezekiel, God comforted the exiles with visions of re-establishment, a new and more glorious temple, the enthronement of David as their king, their enemies defeated, and the Eden privilege restored. These visions of glory communicated one thing to the Jews in exile—*God has not, nor will He forsake the remnant of his people.*

The New Remnant and Vindication

There has always been a faithful remnant of God's people. If these three servants represent Israel in Jesus' day, then the faithfulness of the two servants represents the remnant. Imagine that you are one of the twelve disciples and just learned that your world and all that has identified you as God's people are destined to be destroyed by a nation of God-hating pagans. Furthermore, your people, who are lovers of God and his Messiah, will become refugees and objects of hatred wherever you flee. Would you not desperately want to hear words of hope and reassurance that your faith is not in vain and that God's truth will be vindicated?

This appears to be Jesus's aim as he finishes his discourse with the disciples in Matthew 25:31–34. He promises a future day when he will sit as Judge on a throne of heavenly glory, judging the nations:

All the nations will be gathered before him, and he will separate the people one from another as a shepherd separates the sheep from the goats. He will put the sheep on his right and the goats on his left. Then the King will say to those on his right, "Come, you who are blessed by my Father; take your inheritance, the Kingdom prepared for you since the creation of the world."

Just as Jeremiah, Daniel, and Ezekiel comforted the remnant of their people with assurances from God that he had not forsaken them, the disciples of Jesus and the remnant of their generation—who would become Christians—needed to hear that God would not forsake them when Rome destroyed Jerusalem. Though their tear-filled eyes will witness the end of an age and the destruction of the Temple, the Kingdom of God will remain as their inheritance, just as it had been promised. Inheriting the Kingdom is a Jewish euphemism for eternal life. There is nothing fundamentally new here. These words of comfort and warning are spoken to remind them of the promise of God that says, "for the LORD your God goes with you; he will never leave you nor forsake you" (Deut. 31:6b)

Conclusion

The Jewish leadership that daily recited the *Shema* may have declared their acceptance of the Reign of God, but their violent actions did not match their whitewashed words. They buried their assignment of the love-mandate. Jesus will say to them at the final judgment, "Depart from me, you who are cursed, into the eternal fire prepared for the devil and his angels" (Matt. 25:41). But he will say to those who invested his assignment, "Well done, good and faithful servant! You have been faithful with a few things; I will put you in charge of many things. Come and share your master's happiness!" (Matt. 25:21, 23)

Wrapping Up Our Study

The Kingdom Parables of Christ present several challenges for us when they are treated outside of their Jewish background. Studying these parables without appreciating their Jewish setting leaves them open to allegorizing and misinterpretation, causing our interpretation of the Kingdom of God to suffer. Suppose we discuss the Kingdom of God properly by considering the nuances of early Jewish concepts of the Kingdom, which shaped and formed Jewish expectations of the coming new age and the Messiah. These subtleties provide the seedbed for the Kingdom Parables. Without this approach, shades of meaning within Jewish phrases and images of each parable are otherwise missed. Can we gain valuable knowledge and understanding from these parables without knowing the Jewish context embedded within them? Yes, absolutely, but we must do more than merely acknowledge the Jewish qualities that form the foundation of these Hebrew parables.

I hope we have seen that our institutionalized Western concept of the Kingdom is too limited. While it is true that not every first-century Jewish notion of the Kingdom was correct, the Jews correctly viewed the Kingdom of Heaven in a multidimensional way. The Reign of God was viewed as an active Divine Presence combined with an expectation of something more glorious to come. This is precisely what Jesus demonstrated through his Kingdom Parables.

This multidimensional quality of the Kingdom makes the Kingdom of God genuinely amazing. Substantiated with scripture, we have seen that the Kingdom of God has always been spoken of in past, present, and future tenses and as a Kingdom that rules over all. Jesus expanded on these Kingdom concepts in his parables by illustrating the Reign of God through everyday life. Using familiar images like a man sowing seed, finding treasure in a field, a woman making bread, weddings and banquets, and a king pardoning a thieving servant, the Kingdom Parables depict the Reign of God as accessible, obtainable, empowering, and imposing. There is hope for those who choose to walk by faith in God; for those who do not heed these teachings, there is only warning.

The Kingdom Parables teach us that living within the Reign of God cannot be separated from observing the Shema and its twin commandment. How can we claim to be people of the Kingdom without a daily, conscientious acceptance of what the Shema encompasses? For this reason, the Messiah deliberately and skillfully interweaves the requirement to love God holistically and to love your neighbor as yourself throughout the Kingdom Parables. Jesus intended to underscore and remind us how the Reign of God is expressed. The commandment that fulfills them all becomes the foundation for the Kingdom Parables. Finally, Jesus intends for us to invest in the reign of God by letting God reign in us rather than burying our kingdom assignment.

One Thing More

Suppose we claim to trace our spiritual roots and foundation back to that Pentecost day when Jesus poured out his Spirit to inaugurate a new covenant and sanctify a new creation in Israel. In that case, we must recognize the church of Christ as the Kingdom of Heaven restored to Israel. I have included this discussion in the following chapter, expanding previous discussions so prominent in the Kingdom Parables. So, please read on. May God bless your study of his reign and rule in the world and your life, which are powerfully illustrated by parables sown in Jewish soil.

Food for Thought

1. From a Jewish viewpoint, what would this parable emphasize?

2. Who does the one-talent man represent?

3. Discuss who the faithful servants represent.

4. How does Jesus reassure the faithful that their faithfulness will be vindicated? Discuss how this compares to the prophets' reassurance of the remnant in their day.

5. Discuss how the *Shema* and loving your neighbor as yourself are regarded as acts of worship to the Messiah.

6. What acts of love express God's reign in his people and thereby become marks of identity?

7. What is the most meaningful thing you learned from this lesson?

Part 4

Chapter 23

The Kingdom of the Messiah Is the Restored Kingdom of Israel

I want to acknowledge Jim McGuiggan, whose teaching on *the Reign of God* has broadened my understanding of the Kingdom of God in the Messiah. Previously, I explained how necessary it is to understand the nature of the Kingdom to place a correct perspective on the Kingdom Parables. In chapter three, *The Jewish Concept of the Kingdom,* it was pointed out that the Jews expected God's reign to be revealed in the new age that would also bring the King of Israel, the Messiah. One view of the Kingdom of Heaven was nationalistic and political while involving all of humanity. But more than anything, they believed the Kingdom would be restored to Israel. From the fourth chapter, *The Reign of God in the Old Testament,* we learned that Jesus was not introducing a different or new kingdom, but the one and only Kingdom of God that rules over all. This study will help us see where Christ's church is the promised, expected, and restored Kingdom to Israel.

The Eternal Kingdom

The fact that the Kingdom of God never had a beginning poses something of a dilemma for some of us when we read Daniel 2:44, where he predicts that God will *set up* an everlasting Kingdom during the time of a later kingdom illustrated by the image of Nebuchadnezzar's dream. Daniel 2:44 reads, "In the time of those kings, the God of heaven will set up a kingdom that will never be destroyed, nor will it be left to another people. It will crush all those kingdoms and bring them to an end, but it will itself endure forever." We now know that the "time of those kings" was the Roman Empire since this is the kingdom that followed the Greek Empire. Daniel prophesied that the eternal Kingdom would be set up during this historical period.

Here is the question that arises from this dilemma. How can God's Kingdom be established or set up if it has always existed? To suggest that it existed in the mind of God but was not established on earth until Christ's resurrection does not agree with what is taught concerning the Kingdom in the Old Testament. The Hebrew Scriptures teach that the Reign of God was in the earth from the beginning. "Your kingdom is an everlasting kingdom, and your dominion endures **through all generations,**" David writes in Psalm 145:13a (emphasis mine). Furthermore, to say that the Kingdom was postponed, leaving the "church age" as a substitute until Christ returns at some future time to establish his Kingdom, is likewise failing to interpret Kingdom passages of the Bible correctly. The Reign (Kingdom) of God has always been present *on earth,* not to mention that it existed before the world was created and will never end.

To help answer what is meant by *setting up* the Kingdom, we need to consider a question directed to Jesus in Acts 1:6. The apostles asked, "Lord, will you at this time restore the Kingdom to Israel?" Luke records the apostles asking this question to the risen Messiah before his ascension. This was at the end of forty days of intermittent appearances of the Lord with hundreds of his disciples (1 Cor. 15:3–6). During this period, Jesus spoke more plainly about the nature of the Kingdom of God than before. Something in what Jesus said caused them to ask this curious question about the *restoration* of the Kingdom rather than the setting up of the Kingdom—unless *setting up* and *restoration* speak of the same thing.

Many have assumed that the apostles did not know what they were asking, as at other times, they did not know when they asked questions. The assumption is that the question bears the same nationalistic view of the Kingdom common among most first-century Jews. However, there is a good indication that their curiosity was precise, appropriate, and without previous misconceptions. How can we know? First, notice that Jesus did not correct the substance of their question. Instead, he told them that the *time* of the restoration of the Kingdom was not theirs to know. This answer seems strange if their question had no basis in reality or truth. So we might ask, "What *was* theirs to know?" *God would restore the Kingdom to Israel.*

By this time, the apostles had an opportunity to be with Jesus during forty amazing days after his resurrection. During that time, Jesus was "speaking of the things pertaining to the Kingdom of God" (Acts 1:3). Luke tells us that Jesus had "opened their understanding, that they might comprehend the scriptures."[17] The Scriptures here are the Hebrew Scriptures that tell of the coming Messiah and his reign. Though the Holy Spirit would be needed to finish the specifics of the revelation for the Apostles (cf. John 14:26; 16:13), this says that Jesus gave them a complete understanding of the nature of the Kingdom. While some questions would remain unanswered, their concept of the Kingdom and its restoration were becoming more apparent. Therefore, their question appears more informed and appropriate, lacking former misconceptions. Let's work through what we know from Scripture.

The Eternal Throne

The eternal Kingdom must have an eternal throne. This prompts us to question what the *setting up* of the Kingdom, as predicted by Daniel, and the establishment of the Kingdom, as foretold by Samuel and others, truly mean. Is this the same as restoring the Kingdom to Israel? We need to examine God's promises to King David to answer this question.

Israel was given special status regarding the Reign of God, beginning with the promise to Abraham, but this was not realized until the time of Moses. This special status as God's elect distinguished them from the other nations. They were also given special privileges, such as setting up a physical representative of the true King, the Holy One of Israel. The physical reign of David, Solomon, and their descendants symbolized the eternal throne—imperfect as they were.

David, the son of Jesse, was the first Judean king whom God had foreordained. He would have been king even if King Saul, a Benjamite

(Israel's first king), had not failed. Saul was nothing more than a pacifier for a childish nation until God's appointed time.[18] David had many sons by several wives and concubines, but before his death, Solomon, the son of Bathsheba, was selected as the third king of Israel. When Solomon ascended to the throne, it is said that he sat on *the throne of the* LORD. "So Solomon *sat on the throne of the* LORD as king in place of his father David" (1 Chron. 29:23, emphasis mine). If God's throne is eternal, then the throne of David is likewise eternal.

The Eternal Covenant

God made a covenant with David, which stands today as an everlasting covenant. This eternal covenant promised to enthrone one of David's descendants, saying, "Your house and your kingdom will endure forever before me; your throne will be established forever" (2 Sam. 7:11–16; cf. Acts 2:30–31). However, it came with privileges and consequences. Psalm 89 outlines these conditional terms. The covenant with David and his descendants contained punitive clauses if the terms were violated (Psalm 89:38–39). It was not long until the kings of Israel and Judah violated these terms. King Solomon was the first to violate them. As God had warned, because of the sins of the kings of Israel and Judah, the crown was eventually removed. King Zedekiah was the last king of Judah to be dethroned (2 Kings 25:7). For almost 600 years, there would not be a descendant of David seated as king of Israel. Governors and High Priests filled the void, serving as heads of the nation.

However, even though the monarchy was removed, the throne remained securely eternal and occupied by the Holy One of Israel from above. God promised he would restore the throne of David and make the Kingdom even more glorious than before. To establish that God intended to restore the Kingdom to Israel, the Book of Daniel was written to reassure Judah during the Babylonian exile and the Intertestamental period. The exiles needed to know that the covenant to David had not been, nor would be, overthrown by the removal of the Judean kings nor by the Gentile dominations of the Babylonians, Persians, Greeks, and Romans. Likewise, the prophecy of Ezekiel was used to strengthen the faith of the captives in Babylon by foretelling the restoration of the throne of David. God promised, "My servant David will be king over them, and they will all have one shepherd. They will follow my laws and be careful to keep my decrees" (Ezek. 37:24). Ezekiel was not speaking of a period in some future millennial kingdom. He was speaking of the same days mentioned in Daniel 2:44 to be fulfilled by the enthronement of the Messiah during the period of the Roman Empire. An eternal covenant backed this promise. It would be a new covenant, Jeremiah predicted, that would govern the eternal Kingdom with the Messiah as King.

The Remnant of Israel and the Kingdom of God

The Kingdom of God, the throne, and the covenant are eternal. The role that the remnant of Israel played in restoring the Kingdom is very important. The remnant served faithfully in at least three ways: (1) The remnant of Israel served as the human vessel through whom the Messiah would enter the world; (2) The remnant of Israel served as God's ambassador to the nations as his herald announcing the coming of the King and Kingdom; and (3) The remnant of Israel served as the *realm* through which God demonstrated his *reign* among the nations.

Through the remnant of Israel, the restoration of the Kingdom would be realized for all nations. God never intended for the Kingdom to be restored as an independent or nationalistic kingdom but instead as a Kingdom for all the nations. However, as we can see from Paul's defense of what God had accomplished, the restored Kingdom was not what some expected. The Book of Romans is Paul's thesis on the Kingdom's vindication of the righteousness of God, for which the remnant of Israel had long awaited. Regrettably, for Paul, many Jews rejected Jesus as their Messiah, leading him to declare, "They are not all Israel who are of Israel" (Rom. 9:6).

He goes on to establish the restored Kingdom's universal multi-ethnicity while maintaining and emphasizing the significance of its Hebrew roots. The multi-ethnic quality within the restored Kingdom of Israel is erased by being absorbed into the remnant of Israel since all are now one in Christ (Gal. 3:28–29; Eph. 2:13–16). Paul illustrates this through the metaphor of an ancient olive tree whose branches are both

Jew and Gentile. The Jews are the natural branches, while the Gentiles are the engrafted branches. They are both supported by the same trunk and root firmly established in Hebrew soil. Through the remnant of Israel, God ensured that the Kingdom of the Messiah would be the Kingdom of David restored to Israel.

To say that the cross of Christ and the salvation of the Gentiles was a divine conspiracy designed to doom the Jewish people for rejecting Jesus as the Messiah is simply unscriptural. The notion that was perpetuated by some in the early Gentile church, saying that God abandoned the Jews who composed the remnant of Israel, is a mistaken one as well. Unfortunately, it is an idea that prevails even today. As Anthony Saldarini correctly observes in his examination of the Gospel of Matthew, "There is no covert reference to the Gentiles replacing Israel or Israel being separated from Jesus" (42). The Gentiles and the remnant of Israel are joined together in the same Kingdom and Messiah.

Establishing and Restoring the Kingdom to Israel

We saw from chapter four, *The Reign of God in the Old Testament*, that the Old Testament teaches God's Kingdom as a multidimensional Kingdom. His rule is eternal, having neither a beginning nor an end. His Kingdom rules over all. Yet, Daniel prophesied that it would be *set up* at a later time, which we now understand as the enthronement of the resurrected Messiah during the period of the Roman Empire. Was this a prediction of the passing away of an old Kingdom of God and replaced by a new Kingdom of God?

Let's examine what we know. The New Testament reveals to us that Jesus is the rightful King who inherited the throne of his ancestor, David. It is from and through this eternal throne that he exercises his sovereign rule in heaven and on earth today. However, we still have to address the question of how the Kingdom of God could be set up or established when it already existed. Isn't this a contradiction, or an impossibility?

Jesus and the writers of the New Testament teach without question the deity of Jesus who always existed (cf. John 1:1–14). There has never been a moment when he was not God and thus, King of kings. John testifies that the One whom Isaiah saw seated on a throne high and lifted up was the pre-incarnate Messiah (John 12:41). Yet, there is a part of his being that did not always exist. The Son of God had to become the Son of Man.

The establishment of the Messianic Kingdom, as predicted by Samuel and the prophets, referred to the restoration of the Kingdom to Israel and the revelation of Jesus as the enthroned and glorified God-Man, the Son of David. He has always been the enthroned King, but this new revelation could not have been established before the incarnation of Jesus and his resurrection from the dead. His reign as the Son of Man could not have been set up without his bodily resurrection. The restoration of the Davidic Kingdom to Israel under a new covenant was inaugurated and proclaimed. This was new.

A New Creation

When we speak of the Kingdom being restored to Israel, we are referring to Israel as a new creation. In this New Creation, the Gentiles are added according to the same terms as the Jews, thereby canceling any distinction between the two. Since the Day of Pentecost, a new identity was revealed for those who believe and are baptized into Christ. This newly established identity is in his church where we are able to share in Israel's heritage as children of Abraham and heirs according to the promise.

Therefore, what was established or set up is simply the enthronement of David's descendant, Jesus of Nazareth, who is the resurrected and glorified Man. It speaks of the restoration of the eternal Kingdom to Israel under the rule of the Messiah and governed by a new and eternal covenant. The body of Christ became the *restoration of the Kingdom* that Peter asked about and, therefore, the full expectation of Israel. Again, this is what was new.

The Kingdom of God and the throne are eternal. The new covenant of the Kingdom is eternal. Jesus has always been the King and the Lord of Hosts. When he became human, died, was buried, raised from death, and enthroned, the eternal kingdom, the one that has always existed, became the Messianic Kingdom that was established in Israel and set up in the days of the Roman Empire. Therefore, we are not talking about a new Kingdom of God, but a new arrangement for the Kingdom of God that has always existed.

Food for Thought

1. Discuss why it is logical to assume that the disciples' question was an informed one, and not like previous misunderstandings of the Kingdom.

2. How is the throne of David described in 1 Chronicles 29:23?

3. List the three ways the remnant served faithfully throughout Israel's history.

4. How does Paul illustrate the relationship of the Gentiles and the remnant of Israel from

5. Romans 11.

6. Discuss how the Kingdom of Christ and the throne of David are the same.

7. Discuss how the church of Christ is the full expectation of Israel or the restored Kingdom of Israel.

8. Discuss how the Kingdom of God can be eternal and have qualities of a new creation.

9. What is the most meaningful thing you learned from this study?

10. What is the most meaningful thing you learned from this lesson?

Bibliography

Arias, Mortimer. 1984. *Announcing the Reign of God.* Lima: Fortress.

Bailey, Kenneth. 1976. *Poet and Peasant.* Grand Rapids: Eerdmans.

———. 1980. *Through Peasant Eyes.* Grand Rapids: Eerdmans.

Barclay, William. 1958. *The Gospel of Matthew.* vol. 2. Philadelphia: Westminster.

Beasley-Murray, George R. 1986. *Jesus and the Kingdom of God.* Grand Rapids: Eerdmans.

Brenton, Sir Lancelot C. L. *English Translation of the Septuagint Bible Online.* 1851. http://www.ecmarsh.com/lxx/

Dodd, C. H. 1961. *The Parables of the Kingdom.* New York: Charles Scribner's Sons.

Evans, Craig A. 2000. "Parables in Early Judaism" ed. Richard N. Longenecker. *The Challenge of Jesus' Parables.* Grand Rapids: Eerdmans.

Ferguson, Everett. 1987. *Backgrounds of Early Christianity.* Grand Rapids: Eerdmans.

———. 1979. "Christian Use of the Old Testament." *The World and Literature of the Old Testament.* The Living Word Commentary. vol.1. ed. John T. Willis. Austin: Sweet .

———. 1996. *The Church of Christ: A Biblical Ecclesiology for Today.* Grand Rapids: Eerdmans.

Flanary, Sammy. 2005. *The Holy Spirit: Power, Baptism, Indwelling.* Lubbock: Sunset Institute.

Fosdick, Henry E. 1950. *The Man from Nazareth.* London: SCM Press LTD.

France, R.T. 1990. *Divine Government: God's Kingship in the Gospel of Mark.* Vancouver: Regent College.

Fruchtenbaum, Arnold. 2005. *The Three Messianic Miracles.* San Antonio: Ariel Ministries.

Herzog II, William R. 1994. *Parables as Subversive Speech: Jesus as Pedagogue of the Oppressed.* Louisville: Westminster John Knox.

Hunter, Archibald M. 1960. *Interpreting the Parables.* Philadelphia: Westminster.

Jeremias, Joachim. 1963. *The Parables of Jesus.* Revised Edition. New York: Charles Scribner's Sons.

Jewish Encyclopedia. "Salt: Symbolic Use—In Rabbinical Literature and Jewish Life." http://www.jewishencyclopedia.com/view.jsp?artid=94&letter=S&search=Salt%20 symbolic%20use#375.html

Kearley, F. Furman. 1986. *Biblical Interpretation: Principles and Practices.* F. Furman Kearley, eds. al. Grand Rapids: Baker.

Lightfoot, John. 1979. *A Commentary on the New Testament from the Talmud and Hebraic.* vol. 2. Peabody: Hendrickson.

Lightfoot, Neil R. 1965. *Lessons from the Parables.* Grand Rapids: Baker

McGuiggan, Jim. 1992. *The Reign of God: A Study of the Kingdom of God.* Fort Worth: Star Bible.

_____. 1993. "Parables." International Video Bible Lessons: *Exploring the Bible Text and Related Topics.* Houston: Gospel Services, Inc.

Moseley, Ron. 1996. *Yeshua: A Guide to the Real Jesus and the Original Church.* Baltimore: Lederer.

Oesterley, W.O.E. 1936. *The Gospel Parables in the Light of Their Jewish Background.* London: SPCK.

Saldarini, Anthony J. 1994. *Matthew's Christian-Jewish Community.* Chicago: Chicago Press.

Shulam, Joseph. 1997. *A Commentary on the Jewish Roots of Romans.* Baltimore: Lederer.

Stern, David H. 1992. *.Jewish New Testament Commentary.* Clarksville: Jewish New Testament.

Stern, Frank. 2006. *A Rabbi Looks at Jesus' Parables.* Lanham: Rowman and Littlefield.

Thayer, Joseph Henry. 1966. Fifth Printing. *Greek—English Lexicon of the New Testament.* Grande Rapids: Zondervan.

Young, Brad H. 1989. *Jesus and His Jewish Parables: Rediscovering the Roots of Jesus' Teachings.* Mahwah: Paulist.

_____. 1995. *Jesus the Jewish Theologian.* Peabody: Hendrickson.

———. 1998. *The Parables: Jewish Tradition and Christian Interpretation.* Peabody: Hendrickson.

Wenham, David. 1989. *The Parables of Jesus.* Downers Grove: Intervarsity.

Westermann, Claus. 1990. *The Parables of Jesus in the Light of the Old Testament.* Minneapolis: Fortress.

Whiston, William. 1960. trans. *Josephus: Complete Works.* vol. 1–4. Grand Rapids: Kregal

Willis, John T. 1980. *Isaiah.* gen. ed. John T. Willis. ed. David G. Jones. The Living Word Commentary. vol. 12. Austin: Sweet.

Wilson, Marvin R. 1989. *Our Father Abraham: Jewish Roots of the Christian Faith.* Grand Rapids: Eerdmans.

Wylen, Stephen M. 1996. *The Jews in the Time of Jesus: An Introduction.* Mahwah: Paulist.

———. 2005. *The Seventy Faces of Torah.* Mahwah: Paulist.

Endnotes

1   Regarding riddles, Jeremias argues from the Hebrew *mashal*, that *parabolais* translated parables in Mark 4:11b, should be understood as referring to riddles, thus more accurately resembling the Hebrew *mashal* than the Greek parable. Riddles are intended to obscure. He believes the present translation of Mark 4:11 leaves the opportunity open for misinterpretation. His translation of this passage reads, "To you has God given the secret of the Kingdom of God; but to those who are without everything is obscure, in order that they (as it is written) may 'see and yet not see, may hear and yet not understand, unless they turn and God will forgive them.'" Jeremias concludes that this saying is referring to the preaching of Jesus in general, rather than his parables per se. "The secret of the Kingdom is disclosed to the disciples, but to the outsiders the words of Jesus remain obscure because they do not recognize his mission nor repent. Thus for them the terrible oracle of Isa.6:9f is fulfilled. Yet a hope still remains: 'if they repent God will forgive them.'" (Jeremias, *The Parables of Jesus*, 17–18)

2   A simile contains a stated likeness (for example, "The Kingdom of heaven is like …")

3   Joseph Shulam, *A Commentary on the Jewish Roots of Romans*, 7. "Midrash is a comprehensive term for the Jewish exegesis of Scripture and individually collected works of Scriptural interpretation … It also refers to a specific mode of interpretation, based primarily on 'verbal analogy' in which one Scriptural text is interpreted through a second (cf. Paul's use of Ps. 32:1–2 in order to interpret Gen.15:6)." Shulam, *Ibid.*, p.x.

4   Bill R. Day, *The Moses Connection*, 10–11, quoting Neal Pryor, "The Use of the Old Testament in the New." *Biblical Interpretation: Principles and Practices.* F. Furman Kearley, eds. *et al.*, 276.

5   Everett Ferguson, *Christian Use of the Old Testament, The World and Literature of the Old Testament,* The Living Word Commentary, I:374.

6   Frank Stern, *A Rabbi Looks at Jesus' Parables*, 14. (*pardeys* in Aramaic—an acronym made up of the first letter of *peshat, remez, derash* and *sod* = PaR-DeyS)

7   *Song Rabbah*, 1:1. Quoted by Craig A. Evans, "Parables in Early Judaism," *op. cit.*, 73.

8   For a more thorough reading on this, I highly recommend *The Moses Connection* by Bill R. Day.

9   Jim McGuiggan, "Parables," International Video Bible Lessons: Exploring the Bible Text and Related Topics.

10   It is interesting that in the Old Testament, when Israel repeatedly turned away from God their unfaithfulness was described by a related word in Hebrew, *zonah*, which is the word for "prostitute."

11   Midrashim, Yalkut Shimeon I, 140 quoted by Brad H. Young, *The Parables: Jewish Tradition and Christian Interpretation*, 285–6.

12   The healing in his "wings" prophesies of Jesus' healing power. The corners of a Jewish prayer shawl were called "wings." People were healed by the mere touch of the corner of his shawl (Matthew 9:20; 14:36).

13   Jewish Encyclopedia, "Salt: Symbolic Use in Rabbinical Literature and Jewish Life, http://jewishencyclopedia.com/view.jsp?artid=94&letter=S&search=Salt%20 symbolic%20use#375.html

14   The Babylonian Talmud is a collection of rabbinic elaborations on the Mishnah. The Talmud was not completed until about 500 B.C. The lesser influential collection of writings is the Palestinian Talmud which is dated around 300 B.C.

15   John 1:7 says, "For the law was given through Moses, but grace and truth came through Jesus Christ." This verse is used many times to contrast the difference between the Law of Moses and the grace of the gospel of Christ. The assertion is that the Law was devoid of grace. However, this misses the point. John's point is that, the law was not personified in Moses in the way grace and truth are in Jesus. When the Word became flesh, grace and truth were likewise personified in Jesus Christ. The law was not personified in Moses as grace and truth are in Jesus.

16   An example of this is found in the Dead Sea Scrolls that contain references to a Messianic Banquet. However, it was expected that the Messiah would remain within the existing rules and terms of the Qumran community (1QSa).

17   Luke 24:45 with John 20:22. John records the same appearance of Jesus as recorded in Luke 24:36–43. When Jesus said, "Receive the Holy Spirit," He gave them inspiration necessary to understand all the prophecies concerning Himself and the nature of the Kingdom. This gets into the question of apostolic inspiration prior to Pentecost. However, the apostles had already experienced the empowering of the Spirit prior to this time (cf. Matt. 10:5ff, which should not make this seem that unusual.)

18   God's appointment of Saul, son of Kish, a Benjamite, was a stop-gap measure to prevent Israel from slipping into idolatry. By asking for a king in order to be like the nations around them, they were asking for someone other than God to worship. The pagan kings deified themselves. To their people, they were gods. This might give a better understanding of God's words to Samuel who felt dejected. "And the LORD told him: 'Listen to all that the people are saying to you; it is not you they have rejected, but they have rejected me as their king" (1 Samuel 8:7).

www.ingramcontent.com/pod-product-compliance
Lightning Source LLC
Chambersburg PA
CBHW042135160426
43200CB00019B/2945